MW01484750

For the Love of Literature

Teaching Core Subjects with Literature

By Maureen Wittmann

Ecce Homo Press
La Grange, KY

To my daughter Mary, who is a blessing in more ways
than she can ever know.

Other items available through Ecce Homo Press:

Little Flower Girls Club Leaders and Members Guides
Wreaths I-IV
By Rachel Watkins

Blue Knights Boys' Club Leader and Members Guides
Years One through Four
By Dan McGuire

Glory of America! Catholic Boys and Girls ofthe USA!
The Orphans Find a Home, a St. Francis Xavier Cabrini Story
Kat Finds a Friend, a St. Elizabeth Ann Seton Story
Thomas Finds a Treasure, a St. John Neumann Story
Willy Finds Victory, a Blessed Francis Seelos Story
By Joan Stromberg

And
Jose Finds a King, a Blessed Miguel Pro Story
By Ann Ball

Call toll free for your free catalog:
1-866-305-8362

on the web:
www.eccehomopress.com

Table of Contents

In Appreciation

To Joan Stromberg, not only as my publisher but also as my friend. She believed in this book and was incredibly patient with me as I worked to complete it.

To Joe Stromberg, who took my manuscript and formatted it so that you, the reader, may better enjoy it.

To Mike Aquilina Jr., who encouraged me a great deal from the book's inception to its completion.

To Nancy Carpentier Brown and Mary Jo Thayer. When I found myself overwhelmed with proofreading, Nancy and Mary Jo came to my rescue, and without hesitation. Nancy also lent her expertise on G. K. Chesterton and helped with some of the book descriptions.

To the reviewers on the board of Favorite Resources for Catholic Homeschoolers, including Mary Daly, Margot Davidson, MacBeth Derham, Mary Gildersleeve, Suchi Myjak, Maria Rioux, Alicia Van Hecke, and Beth Yank, who offered help with the reading lists. They also helped with the "Charlotte Mason" and "Classical Education" chapters.

To Becky Wissner who suggested the "At a Glance" chapter.

To Rachel Mackson who suggested listing the country of origin with each literary recommendation.

To my aunt, Dr. Patty Fagin, principal of Villa Duchesne School, for reading my preliminary manuscript and offering much needed insights.

To the library clerks and librarians at the main branch of the Capital Area District Library, who always make themselves available when I need help searching out books and never scold me when I leave with forty or fifty books a library trip, especially Ann Lucas and Heather Goupil. I'd also like to thank Cassie Veselovsky, the children's librarian, for setting aside time to explain to me how homeschoolers can work hand in hand with their librarians.

To my friends and family members who, over the years, have shared with me their advice and ideas about children's literature. Especially my sister Chris Statler, my friends Linda Biewer, Amy DallaVecchia, Sheila Pohl, Sonya Romans, Linda Skiba, Dawn Smith, the mothers on CHSL, and the women on all my favorite email groups. They encourage me to keep up the search for great books to feed my children.

To the teenagers in Readers' Anonymous, Paul, Jeffry, Rebekah, Rebecca, Mary, Christian, Olivia, Joshua, Jacob, Austin, and all the rest. I've learned far more from this group of high school students than I could ever dreamed of teaching them.

To my children, who are my inspiration. They are a great blessing.

To my husband and best friend, Rob, for loving me just as God made me.

Finally, but most importantly, to God Almighty for His many gifts.

Foreword

Mike Aquilina, Jr.

My father raised his seven children to have a deep reverence for books. "Our books," he often told us, "are our friends."

In his own childhood, in the 1920s and '30s, books were a rarity, like oranges and grapefruits, a luxury indulged by the families of the men who *owned* the mines, not the men who *worked* the mines. My father's father, an immigrant and coal miner, died in 1926 from complications of black lung, leaving my grandmother with no money and seven children to raise.

But my grandfather had left his children something valuable. He left them the memory of seeing their own Papa read and write. In their neighborhood, a little Sicilian-American ghetto, Calogero was one of the few immigrants who could read and write, and he could read and write in both English and Italian. Thus he was an invaluable asset to the community. He was the man who could help families with their immigration papers. He was the man who could write letters home to Sicily. He was the man who could read the letters they received from the *Americani* immigration authorities.

Calogero's children knew from an early age that reading could confer a certain nobility, even upon the poorest of the poor. Their father owned nothing, but he was a man of stature in the patch. When he died, his funeral procession (according to news reports) included seventy-three cars and more than a thousand people. Five full cars held only flowers. And, long after he died, grown men would tip their hats whenever my father or his siblings walked by.

This didn't pay the bills, though; and, with the Great Depression, life got even harder. But my father found, then, that reading could also provide a means of

9

escape. The stories he read in school took him far from his family's difficulties, to lands across the ocean and times long past. Pop and his friends started a club, with dues of one cent per member per month. With their treasury, they would buy a dime novel, and pass it around in the course of the month. It wasn't high culture. The patch boys were big on Alexandre Dumas — *The Count of Monte Cristo*, *The Three Musketeers*. But in those pages they could learn to find a little romance, even in poverty, and hope for something better.

And his hopes were fulfilled in time. The year before he died, he wrote to me that he was "richer than Bill Gates."

What made my father rich, and what made his father noble, was not their money in the bank. They had none. What made them rich and noble was a capacity to love that they acquired, at least in part, through reading.

Books are like conversation. They can help us to enter imaginatively into a world we would not otherwise know. They can help us transcend our cramped horizons and see how others live, and how they suffer, and how they endure. What we meet first in books, we can more readily recognize in life. We can notice a need in the neighborhood — someone living in loneliness, grief, or abuse –– because it's all familiar from fairy tales. And often, from the same children's stories, the proper response is clear to us.

Reading is a pleasure and a joy; it's an escape and a diversion; it's edifying and inspiring. But, when it's really good, it's still more than that. It's all about love. My grandfather placed his literacy at the service of the poor around him, even though he was very poor himself. My father wished to do the same.

This is what Maureen Wittmann is teaching us with this book, and with everything else she does as an educator

10

and a mother. Today, books are hardly a rarity, as they were in my father's childhood. But kids disdain them. Think of all the opportunities they're missing — to meet people from long ago and far away; to feel that certain heartbreak at the end of a book, even if it has a happy ending, because you know you'll never see your favorite character again.

But you will, because that character has changed you, made you more ready to love, more ready to serve, more ready to find the same story played out in the place where you live.

Our books, indeed, are our friends. Maureen Wittmann helps us to cultivate a lifetime of great friendships.

Introduction

"Christian, how did you get to be such a good writer?"

"Because you always give me good books to read, like *Lord of the Rings*."

At 13, my son Christian hated to write. It was one of those struggles between mother and son I thought would never be resolved. Every writing assignment given to him was met with disdain. As a result, my husband and I were beginning to rethink our pedagogical approach. Maybe I was wrong, as my children's teacher, to put so much emphasis on real books and so little on textbooks. As my husband wisely pointed out: It's not enough to read great books; one must be able to communicate the book's lessons. In college, my son would be required to write thesis papers and, at the rate we were going, I couldn't see how he was going to make it to that point. This all changed one day when I did something quite radical.

It began with our history co-op. I required the children in the co-op to read a book every two weeks and follow-up with a book report. My son loved reading the books but hated the book reports. (Perhaps, I should've listened to Andrew Pudewa, of the Institute for Excellence in Writing, who says book reports are one of the most difficult writing assignments to give young children.) Christian would sit in front of a blank screen on the computer with an equally blank look on his face as he struggled to write. I would ask him to tell me about the book and he would do so in great detail. I would then tell him to write exactly what he had just said to me, but he would insist he couldn't. I would then insist he could. After all, if you can talk, you can write. He didn't understand my logic.

Caught up in a moment of inspiration, and tired of

my son's complaints, I told the children one day their history assignment had changed. No more book reports. Instead, they were to write their own book, a piece of historical fiction based on our current studies. They were to choose a Spanish or Portuguese explorer or missionary to the Americas. They were to style their books after Joan Stromberg's Glory of America Series. That is, their books were to be centered on a child protagonist, while still telling the story of the explorer or missionary.

I braced myself for a flurry of protests, but they never came. The children were excited by the new challenge. I assigned anywhere from five to twenty pages, depending on the age of the child. Instead of two weeks, I gave the students a six-week deadline. I promised to lend my desktop publishing experience to show them how to add illustrations, create a cover, and bind the final manuscript.

As soon as co-op was over, Christian called dibs on the computer and typed away until dinnertime. When dinner was finished, he went right back to the computer. After several days of this unusual behavior, I asked if I could read his book up to that point. I found his story to be engaging and interesting. He pulled me right in with the first paragraph. I felt sympathy for his main character, an orphaned boy stowed away on a ship captained by Magellan. I could feel the breeze and smell the musty sails of the ship. I couldn't believe this was written by the same boy who, when given previous writing assignments, would wax endlessly about the torture he was forced to endure.

Once I was able to speak, as I was in a state of shock, I asked Christian how he got to be such a good writer. He told me it was because of the great literature I had fed him through the years. This was like music to my ears. My concerns about his writing skills suddenly evaporated; I was vindicated. Today, my son is seventeen-years

14

old and wants to major in theology and journalism in college. Currently, he is writing his first novel, a fantasy trilogy. Yes, teaching through real books can produce positive results.

In *For the Love of Literature*, I share with you the books I have discovered through my twelve years of homeschooling and in doing research to complete this book. My children or I have read most of the books found in the literary guides. The rest come highly recommended by other Catholic homeschooling parents.

How to Use this Book

For the Love of Literature is meant to be a living book. It should continue to be written and edited . . . by you. When you discover a much-loved book in the literary guides, don't hesitate to highlight it and make notes in the column. If you find a book you dislike, take your red pen and put a line through it. In searching through your library's shelves and in chatting with your friends, you'll discover titles I've missed – add them to the literary guides. Finally, highlight books you already own.

> Notations are provided with each book description to give you an idea of the age appropriateness:
> A: Adult (college age and above)
> H: High school (9th through 12th grade)
> M: Middle school (6th through 8th grade)
> G: Grade school (1st through 5th grade)
> P: Preschool (kindergarten and earlier)
> ✠: Catholic
> *: Discretion advised. Contains adult material.

Every child is different and these are just approximations. Although I have broken the selections into five age groups, they could easily be broken down even further. For example, a high school student in the twelfth grade may be comfortable reading Augustine, while a tenth-grade student may need to wait before tackling such deep works. Then there are books that can be read over a broad age range. For example, there are books that can be enjoyed by both grade school students and middle school students or by both high school students and adults.

If you see a book with both a "G" and an "M," it's probably safe to assume it will work with an upper grade school child as well as a lower middle school child. If you spot a book with a "P" and a "G," then it is likely to work better with your first grade student than your fifth grade student.

Parents are the ultimate authority on the appropriateness of any book for their child. As with anything, please review books before sharing with your children.

With over 950 books listed in the literary guides, you may find yourself overwhelmed. Please know, you and your children are not expected to read all, or anywhere near all, the books I've listed there. Instead, the goal is to give you enough choices from which to pick and choose over the many years you'll be homeschooling. Different children have different tastes and needs. Hopefully, the large number of book choices in the literary guides will provide for each different child.

Though I have broken subjects out separately, they can – and should – be tied all together. For example, math and science often go hand-in-hand. And all subjects can be tied into history, as history is an accounting of everything mankind has accomplished throughout time. (In my home library, I arrange our books in chronological order. This helps the children find the

> ☞ **Valuable Tip**
>
> **Making Geography Part of Your Literature Lessons**
>
> 1. Attach a map to your wall and keep a supply of pushpins close by. Most books will mention one or more locations within the plot line. Have the children find the location(s) on the map and place a pin there. This is especially fun to do with books that take place in many locations such as *Around the World in 80 Days*.
> 2. Always keep a globe handy.
> 3. Find ancient maps online or at the library for books that take place in the ancient world.

books we need as our studies move through history.)

In choosing books for my children, I try to combine multiple subjects. For example, in reading *I, Juan de Pareja* by Elizabeth de Trevino, they will learn about art and history, while at the same time being introduced to the deep Catholic faith of the main character. In reading *Godel, Escher, Bach: An Eternal Golden Braid* by Douglas Hofstadter they will learn about higher mathematics, art, and music. Subjects naturally intertwine in real life. To draw distinct lines between subjects in our homeschools would be doing a disservice to our children. Always look for ways to show children how different disciplines overlap one another.

You will notice I have not included religion as a separate subject. This is because I've made a strong effort to choose books that will raise children's hearts to God through the other subjects. Strive to weave our Catholicism into all school subjects, just as our Catholicism should be woven through our everyday lives.

My sister, who sends her children to a very good private Catholic school, tells me religion is one of her children's most disliked subjects. She believes this is because it's taught like every other school subject, with textbooks, assignments, and tests. Yes, some of this is needed to teach the finer points of our faith, but it should not be done to the point of drill and kill.

We can subtly introduce faith matters through other school subjects. Math teaches order just as God is orderly. Science teaches us this world could not have happened all by itself. We look for moral lessons in literature. We listen to music and view art reflecting God's beauty. We also attend weekday Mass and are involved in various parish ministries. I do some direct instruction in religion. For example, my older children are learning apologetics and my younger children are memorizing their Baltimore Catechism questions and answers. But for the most part, religion is taught in my home through other subjects, and also through the experiential.

You can use *For the Love of Literature* to supplement your homeschool studies or to create your entire curriculum. As a supplement, simply search for books to complement your current studies. For example, if you're studying the Civil War, look in the American history literary guide under the "Civil War" heading.

Using literature as a complete curriculum may require more planning or, at least, more

> ✓ **Checklist**
>
> Book title:
> Subjects covered:
> ☐ Music
> ☐ Art
> ☐ Math
> ☐ Science
> ☐ History
> ☐ Religion
> ☐ Other
> Grade level:___
> Time needed for completion:_____
> Assigned writing project:_____
> Scheduled discussion time:_____

forethought than you are currently giving. One concern parents have with this approach is that their children will be reading more than one book at a time. I don't find this to be a problem. It's not all that different from children working with more than one workbook or textbook at a time. Just as children are able to move from their science textbook to their math textbook to their vocabulary workbook in a single day, so they will be able to move from a science biography to a work of historical fiction to a book on Gregorian chant.

You should either schedule a day and time to discuss assigned books with your student or assign a writing project. This will help you assess his or her understanding of the book(s) and give you the opportunity to further discuss topics.

If you own *The Catholic Homeschool Companion* [Sophia Institute Press], read the essay <u>High School Literary Analysis Made Easy</u> by Carol Maxwell found on pages 117-121. Carol advises parents to use literature guides, such as Cliff Notes, to help develop discussion and writing topics. They can help you come up with all kinds of topics for literary analysis or tests on assigned books. Cliff Notes and other literature guides give a list of characters, glossary, plot outline, background on the author, and more.

For example, when my two oldest children were reading *The Tempest*, Cliff Notes came in quite handy. Shakespeare practically assumes his reader already knows the characters in his play, and it confused my children. Cliff Notes' list of characters describing their part in the plot was helpful in clearing up the confusion.

⌨ **Helpful Websites**

To save on your budget, Cliff Notes can be borrowed from the library. Also, it and other guides can be found online free:
<u>www.cliffnotes.com</u>
<u>www.gradesaver.com</u>
<u>www.novelguide.com</u>
<u>www.sparknotes.com</u>

Hillside Education offers several great Catholic literature guides for sale:
<u>www.hillsideeducation.com</u>

This year my two high school students and I started going out for breakfast on Monday mornings to discuss their current reading projects. Unfortunately, I no longer have the time to read all of the books I assign. This has become more difficult as my little children grow into big children. If I honestly can't find the time to read something I've assigned, I then rely heavily on commercial literature guides to direct our discussions.

How to Use This Book

Some final notes on the literary guides: I've done my best to include only books currently in print. I have discovered many wonderful out-of-print books that could accompany the literary guides; however, searching the Internet and libraries for out-of-print titles takes more time than I'm willing to give. I assume you have the same time constraints. Shortly before *For the Love of Literature* went to the publisher, I checked on each book's availability. (Because books constantly go in and out of print, there will be some that slip through the cracks.)

I also include the names of the publishers for the Catholic books. It was difficult to do this for secular books as quite a few have more than one publisher; besides, they're generally easier to find in libraries and for purchase. For these reasons, I decided not to include the names of the publishers for secular books. Catholic books, on the other hand, are usually published by small publishing houses and can sometimes be difficult to locate. If you have trouble finding any of the Catholic books listed in the literary guides, check the appendix for the website or phone number of the publisher.

The literary guides were difficult to organize with over 950 titles. My goal was to make them easy to use by a homeschooling mother teaching multiple grade levels at one time. Books are separated by topic. Within topic, they are organized by grade level. Within grade level, they are alphabetized.

Using Your Library

It is my hope and prayer this book will help you use literature more extensively in your homeschool. Admittedly, it would be a very expensive, if not impossible, approach if you were to purchase all of the recommended titles. Frequent trips to the library will be necessary if you are to be successful in using literature to teach core subjects.

I save time by using the Internet. I check my library's card catalog online with my reading list in my lap. I also put books on hold at the library website, including inner- and inter-library loans.

Inner-library loans are books borrowed from other branches within the same library district. Inter-library loans are books borrowed from libraries across the state or country. These are important tools for Catholic homeschoolers. Many times the books we desire are older or religious titles, which may be hard to find at our neighborhood library.

At my library, inner- and inter-library loans are easy to obtain through a simple click of a button at the

Using Your Library

> 🖳 **Helpful Website**
>
> ELF: Your Personal Library Reminder Service
> www.libraryelf.com
> If you sign up for this service, and your library is a member, you'll receive regular emails letting you know what you have checked out on your card, what's due when, and the status of any holds, inter-library loans, or inner-library loans. It's especially handy for heavy borrowers and those with multiple cards within one family.

library website. However, every library's system is different. Don't be afraid to ask your librarian to teach you how to use the inner- and inter-library loan options.

A favorite service my library offers is email notification when a book on hold comes in. All I have to do then is run into the library, return the previous week's books, and pick up the books I have waiting. If I'm really busy, I can have my husband pick up my books on his way home from work. If you haven't already, see if your library offers similar services.

Get Organized

Though the library can be a great resource, it's costly if you aren't organized. I usually have more than fifty books checked out at any one time. If I didn't keep proper track of borrowed books, I would be overwhelmed with late fees and lost book charges.

I keep things organized in two ways. First, I keep a log of books I've checked out from the library. Second, I have a designated place in my home for library items.

Keeping a log is very easy for me because my library gives me a receipt of books, videos, and magazines borrowed at check out. This receipt also includes due dates. Additionally, I can go to the library website, check my personal account, and print a list of items currently outstanding. If your library doesn't provide these services, then make up your own log of items borrowed. (See www.maureenwittmann.com for a free download of several library log forms.)

I make sure to check the returned books off my log when I take them back. It's best to mark the actual date returned. Sometimes libraries miss books that have been returned. If my library shows I haven't returned an item, I can look at my log and see if I did indeed forget. If I returned the item, I can notify them of the return date and they put a search on it. It's not that unusual for libraries to shelve a book without first scanning it in. You don't want to waste a day searching needlessly for a book, or worse pay for a lost book, because of a simple clerical error.

The log also doubles as a reading list for your homeschool. It's a good idea to keep track of books read by your children. If you need to create a portfolio, the reading list will be an important addition. At the end of the year, I go over our log to see what we read for the year. This helps me in planning next year's curriculum, and it reassures me my children are doing a great job.

The second thing I do to keep a handle on library books is to have a special place designated for library items only. I have a large wicker basket, which I found for almost nothing at a garage sale. All books, magazines, and videos checked out from the library are to go into this basket. Setting aside a shelf just for library items also works.

Simply doing these two things, and training your children to do them, will save a lot of hassle on library day.

Get Your Library Working for You

Recently, when my parents were visiting from out of state, they accompanied the children and me to the library. As we walked to the children's section, several people stopped us to say hello. My mother asked, "Is there anyone here you don't know?" Probably not.

We spend an incredible amount of time at the library. In fact, a large chunk of this book was written in the library's computer center. But even before I began pulling *For the Love of Literature* together for publication, the children and I visited the library once a week. It didn't take long to find myself on a first-name basis with the librarians and library clerks.

As you get to know the staff at your public library, take advantage of their expertise. That's what they're there for, and it has been my experience library personnel love the opportunity to help their library patrons.

The librarians and library clerks at my library help me find books on particular subjects, as well as show me how to use their website and computer center more efficiently. They've also introduced me to services, such as free meeting rooms, reading groups, and so on. Some libraries also have special privileges for teachers, such as longer checkout periods and higher checkout limits. Ask if such privileges are extended to home educators.

The most beneficial fruit from getting to know my librarians has been having an influence on their book purchasing decisions. Cassie, the children's librarian, has approached me on occasion to seek out my opinion when she has a book order to place. I'm happy to say that I too seek out her advice. It has developed into a friendship based on a love of books.

Cassie shared with me her difficulty in reaching out to schoolteachers. She very much wanted to order the books they assigned to their students. For example, if a teacher assigned *The Red Badge of Courage* to his twenty-five students, and he notified Cassie well enough in advance, she could order extra copies. Then when students came in for the book, it would be available to them and they could complete their assignments on time. Unfortunately, Cassie receives little feedback from schoolteachers. We homeschoolers – home teachers – shouldn't make the same mistake.

Cassie once asked me to go to the homeschooling community and ask for their help in placing a large book order. It was nearing summer time, and she wanted to know what books we needed for the upcoming school year. I reminded Cassie I teach through literature and my book

Using Your Library

order alone would include more than twenty titles. She didn't even blink an eye. In fact, she was greatly enthused by the prospect. I then went to the various homeschooling groups in our community and passed on Cassie's desire for their book requests. In the end, Cassie received hundreds of requests, including some older and obscure titles, and she was able to purchase many of the books.

Making Purchase Requests

You don't have to wait for your library's staff to approach you in order to make purchasing requests. If you avoid using the public library because you don't like their selection, you can do something about it. Libraries have a system in place to take requests from their patrons, and most libraries put a lot of importance on those requests. After all, librarians want to order books that are popular and will be checked out often. They have no desire to see their books sit on a shelf unread.

On average, I make one purchasing request per week and about ninety percent are accepted. This includes blatantly Catholic titles. Don't think because a book is religious it won't find its way to the library's bookshelves.

Conversely, most libraries have a system in place for complaints about specific books. If you find something on the library's shelf you find offensive or inappropriate, you can file a complaint. Recently, a fellow homeschooler did this at her library. She didn't succeed in having the offensive book completely removed from the library, but they did move it from the children's section to the adult section and will think twice before making another similar purchase.

Get to Know the Dewey Decimal Classification System

Knowing the order in which books are shelved at the library will help you and your children a great deal in

📄 Top-Ten Suggestions for Making Purchasing Suggestions to Your Library

10. The form you need to fill out may be called a variety of things: patron request, item request, suggest a purchase, or something similar.

9. Making suggestions online is often easier than filling out a form in person. To find your library's website visit http://lists.webjunction.org/libweb/.

8. Give as much information about the book as you can: title, author, publisher, date published, ISBN number, and a link to a review of the book.

7. Sometimes it's more effective to ask a main library instead of a suburban or branch library.

6. You'll have a better chance of a purchase at a big library than a small one, which needs to get rid of books to save room.

5. Titles published in the past year are more likely to be purchased. Librarians want their purchases to have a long shelf life and so are weary of older books.

4. If you do suggest an older title, make sure to comment it's a "classic" and will be checked out for years to come.

3. Don't give up if you feel your suggestions are ignored. Book orders are made when funds are available, so it may take a few months before you see the fruits of your efforts.

2. Tell all of your like-minded friends to make purchasing suggestions too. Some libraries wait until they have two or three requests of the same book before ordering.

1. Once the library purchases the books you suggest, check them out so the librarian will continue to order similar titles.

searching out desired books, as well as discovering new titles and authors.

For example, when I was desperately searching for math literature, I went to the 500 section at the library, sat down on the floor, and started pulling books off the shelf. In this way, I discovered some real gems.

The Dewey Decimal Classification System is a system used to classify nonfiction books into ten categories. (Fiction books are shelved alphabetically by the author's last name.) The system was invented by a librarian named Melvil Dewey (1851-1931). He also founded the American Library Association, published the first *Library Journal,* and opened the first library school at Columbia University.

Without Mr. Dewey's classification system, libraries would be in chaos. Take time to get to know the system and then teach it to your children. You can either ask your library for help (we once attended a class on Dewey at a neighboring library) or search the Internet.

Library Fees

Unfortunately, some libraries charge excessive fees for their services. They sometimes charge for services such as placing book holds, requesting inter-library loans, or movie rentals. Make sure to check for such fees before using services. You may need to budget for library fees. It's still cheaper to pay a dollar for an inter-library loan than to purchase a book new. But then again, you may be able to borrow a needed book from a friend or purchase it used for little more than the service fee.

Building a Home Library

While the public library is an awesome resource when teaching through literature, it's still important to have a good home library. I would go so far as to say our home library is the center of our homeschool.

Owning books allows for opportunities. Waiting for a trip to the library just isn't the same when a child shows a sudden interest in reading, or you decide to take a rabbit trail off of your current school topic. While I can't afford to buy large quantities of books, I can make sure to buy quality books. For example, I've gone out of my way to purchase the entire Vision series of saint books, Mary Fabyan Windeatt saint biographies, Ecce Homo Press titles, and Bethlehem Books historical fiction.

What's On Your Shelf?

The first step in building a home library is to check what's already on your shelves. You never know what long-forgotten book will be found. Go through your books and get them on your shelves in an orderly fashion. For example, you may want to designate shelves for math, science, art, music, religion, etc. Much like a simplified Dewey Decimal Classification System.

The next step is to check your parents' bookshelves. You may discover

💻 Helpful Websites

My Library Thing
www.librarything.com
This is an online service that allows you to catalog your books online. You can add reviews of books. If you have trouble keeping track of who you've lent books to, then use the handy comment feature. Your book catalog can be private or it can be shared with the world. These are only a few of the My Library Thing's capabilities. The service is free up to 200 books. If you wish to catalog more than 200 the fee is reasonable.

your childhood favorites still residing in your parents' home. If so, bring them to your home to share with your own children. If they were your favorites, they're likely to be your children's favorites too.

Buying Used Books

The next step is to search for quality used books. Library and garage sales are a great start. I've found classic series, from Narnia to Little House, for as little as ten cents each. I've also discovered a few gems at thrift stores, such as St. Vincent DePaul. You'll need to sift through a lot of twaddle to find worthwhile purchases, but that just adds to the fun. Make it an adventure. You can even get your children to help you sift, and in the process, they will learn how to distinguish good books from trash. Take a good reading list with you (*For the Love of Literature*, one of the books in the "Books about Books" chapter, or one of the online reading lists found in the appendix) or a list of favorite authors. This will help you discern what books to buy.

The Internet is also a great source. My favorite Internet resource for used books is CathSwap (www.groups.yahoo.com/group/cathswap/) where more than 2,000 members buy and sell their used Catholic curriculum and books. If you are looking for something in particular, you can send a "Want to Buy" email to the group. When I've done this, I've almost always received a positive response. I've found the prices to be very reasonable and have never had a problem with a seller.

For hard-to-find books, try a website such as www.bookfinder.com. Bookfinder will search the Internet and return to you a list of websites that sell your desired book. This way you can comparison shop in one easy step.

See the appendix for more Internet resources for used books.

Sharing Resources

There will always be a need to purchase new books. In the world of purchasing, there is power in numbers. Schools often save money on curriculum and supplies by combining purchasing orders with other schools. Large orders translate into large discounts. We can imitate this model in our homeschools and support groups.

When it comes time to plan next year's curriculum and you begin ordering books and supplies, consider combining your order with a friend's or, perhaps, your entire homeschooling support group.

Several homeschooling mail order companies offer free shipping and handling when you place an order over a certain dollar amount. The amount can range from $50 to $250. If you don't see free shipping advertised in a favorite vendor's catalog, call or email to inquire. I've always received a positive answer when I've posed this question. I don't know any business that isn't willing to give you a break if you're willing to act as a salesman on their behalf.

Always be aware of shipping and handling costs. I remember being tempted once to order from a company that offered deep discounts on curricula. However, when I added in their over-inflated shipping charges, I found I wasn't saving much money. Since then, whenever possible, I give my business to Catholic homeschooling mail order companies and shy away from businesses promising impossible deals.

Another way to save money is to skip the mail order company and go straight to the publisher. Some publishers will give discounts, on rare occasions as deep as 50%, for bulk orders. If you organize your fellow homeschoolers, you may be able to get enough orders for a great discount.

Years ago, someone in my homeschool support group took orders once a year for a favorite publisher and as a result we enjoyed a 40% discount (plus shipping). It wasn't an easy task. The members collecting the orders and then distributing the books need to be well organized, as well as prepared to put a bit of sweat into the effort.

Every publisher has different rules; therefore, you need to take the initiative to contact your favorite publisher and ask. Some publishers require a purchase of ten books of the same title, while another may simply require that you place a minimum order of $200. Larger publishing houses will probably require you to have an established business and a tax identification number.

Homeschool Lending Library

One of the many blessings of our local homeschool support group is our free lending library, which is especially helpful to new homeschoolers and those investigating homeschooling.

My group's library started in someone's home and then moved to a local parish. The parish is very friendly to homeschoolers and set aside a large space for us in their church library. Someone simply asked the pastor, and his answer was "yes."

All of the books in our library are donated. Generous homeschoolers donate books and texts once they're finish with them, even though they could easily recoup some of their money by selling them used. Also donated are magazines and videos. It's a wonderful resource. Someone simply asked the community for donations and the answer was "yes."

See if you can provide something like this in your homeschooling community. All you have to do is ask.

Reading Aloud

I am a big proponent of reading aloud to children, not only for younger children, but for teenagers as well. In fact, when they get to be teenagers, you can have them read aloud to you or their siblings.

Reading aloud has many benefits. Young children are able to enjoy stories they cannot yet read themselves. In the begining, their reading usually consists of phonics books and easy readers. When cuddling on the couch with Mom or Dad, they can enjoy stories far above the level of *Dick and Jane*. You'll see their vocabularies build as they decode new words heard in stories, and you'll have an easier time teaching them rules of grammar if they are accustomed to hearing proper grammar within their stories. This is why you want to stay away from dumbed-down books and predictable series. Stick to good literature.

Additionally, children always have the opportunity to hear the proper pronunciation of difficult words when hearing a story. Inversely, having children read aloud to you will give you the opportunity to check their pronunciation. (You could even have children read into a tape recorder for later listening.) If your child is having difficulty with certain phonics rules, you'll catch it during their read aloud time and can then go over any trouble spots.

The benefits of reading aloud go beyond academics. We also share the suspense, the fun, the excitement, and the pure emotion. We talk about why we love, or loathe, certain characters or plot lines. It gets us talking to our children about worthwhile topics.

There is also something about getting close to your child while reading. I believe it creates a bond between a parent and child that can't be easily broken. I remember reading *Little Princess* to my six-year-old daughter. We sobbed together as we read the part where the Little

Princess learns her father is dead. In sharing strong emotions through the telling of stories, my daughter will feel comfortable sharing emotions with me in real life situations. Should a boy one day break my daughter's heart, I want her to be comfortable coming to me for a shoulder to cry on. I believe reading aloud sets that stage.

Sharing stories also helps build a love of reading in children. My oldest son was severely dyslexic and didn't take off reading until he was ten-years old. Yet, now as a teenager he absolutely loves to read. One reason for this is that I was able to teach him one-on-one, and he didn't have to experience the difficulty of keeping up with other students. But there is an even bigger reason for his love of books: I read aloud to him more than any of my other children. Because of his learning disability, I had to read all of his books to him for his first ten years. So, this has become part of our relationship and something we just do.

Getting close to one another as you read aloud can't help but make a child feel good, and that good feeling will create a foundation that makes later reading also feel good.

How to Read Aloud in Three Easy Steps

The first step in reading aloud is to find the right book. With small children you'll want to look for colorful and interesting pictures. The rhymes and patterns of language should be like good music, flowing easily. You'll likely be asked to read favorite books over and over again, so make sure the books you choose are easy, as well as enjoyable, for you.

This is true with older children, too. I've read the Chronicles of Narnia to my children countless times and each time was a pleasure. I imagine C. S. Lewis sitting at his typewriter reading aloud as he typed. The words simply flow off your tongue. Conversely, when I attempted to read

The Prince and the Pauper by Mark Twain, it was a dismal failure for us. While a good story, it was incredibly difficult for me to read aloud. The Old English didn't flow well when read by me, a modern American. Plus, I had to stop every few minutes to explain a phrase or define a word. So, the book was put aside to be read silently by the children when they got older.

    The second step is setting the atmosphere. Get comfortable and pull the children close to you. Make sure you have good lighting. There's nothing like having to squint to ruin a lovely evening of reading aloud to the children. And look for a time that is fairly relaxed and quiet. My favorite time to read aloud is in the afternoon, after lunch is finished. (Some people enjoy bedtime, but I'm too tired by then and fall asleep before the children.) If you

---

📄 Top-Ten Reasons to Read Aloud to Your Child

10. Young children can enjoy stories above their reading level.
9. Parents can stop the story to explain difficult concepts or vocabulary.
8. Children can hear the proper pronunciation of difficult words.
7. Parents and children create bonds through the shared emotions of the story.
6. Fosters one-on-one communication between parents and children.
5. Good quality and quantity time between family members.
4. Builds strong vocabularies and good grammar.
3. Improves listening skills.
2. Helps children develop a taste for good literature
1. Excellent alternative to television or video games.

have antsy boys like I do, you can have them sit at your feet and allow them to play as you read. The only requirement is that they're quiet and don't disturb your reading. I found that my bouncing-off-the-wall, ADHD child can sit on the floor playing LEGO's as I read and still comprehend the story.

The third and final step is to use expressive language. Quite honestly, children just want private time with you and won't mind too much if your voice is lifeless, and you just muddle through the story. But why not make your read aloud time more interesting for yourself and more fun for the children? With a little practice you can bring a story to life.

Make words sound like their meaning: BOOM, quiet, squeeeeeeze. Accentuate words to clarify meaning. Make key words louder and emphasize action words (verbs). Also pay attention to the tempo of your story. The Hardy Boys should be read with a fast and exciting tempo. After all, the boys are chasing criminals, dodging trouble, and solving the case. On the other hand, *Little House on the Prairie* would have a slower, easy-going pace. Mary and Laura strolling along through wild roses certainly doesn't require the fast tempo of the Hardy Boys.

Work on developing voices and have some fun with it. While the evil witch will have a deep scratchy voice, Snow White's voice will have a higher pitch that is sweet and tender.

These techniques will come easy with time. Give it a try!

☞ **Valuable Tip**
Three Steps to Reading Aloud
1. Find the right book.
2. Set the atmosphere.
3. Use expressive language.

Classical Education

In 1947 at Oxford University Dorothy Sayers, an English writer and scholar, presented her speech, *The Lost Tools of Learning.* Then in 1977 her speech was published in *National Review* magazine. Since that time, *The Lost Tools of Learning* has been republished countless times.

The "lost tools" of which Miss Sayers spoke were the tools of a classical education. A classical education is based on the Trivium, which is made up of three stages.

The Grammar Stage (grades one to five) builds a foundation by memorizing facts. The Dialectic, sometimes referred to as the Logic Stage, (grades six to eight) develops analytical skills in students. Finally, the Rhetoric Stage (grades nine to twelve) pulls the first two stages together and teaches students the art of articulation

The Trivium is not a modern approach to education. It was developed in the Middle Ages and widely used for centuries. Some say the Trivium is biblically supported. In Proverbs 2:6 we read: "For the Lord gives wisdom: From His mouth come knowledge and understanding." Knowledge, understanding, and wisdom do sound similar to grammar, dialectic, and rhetoric. The Trivium recognizes basic human development. It recognizes how God formed children's intellect.

A classical education is designed to foster a lifelong love of learning. It's not enough to learn facts and ideas; one needs the tools to continue learning after school is out. One needs to continue learning into adulthood. Children taught using the classical model receive the tools of learning – the lost tools spoke of so eloquently in Miss Sayers' speech.

Grammar

A child in the grammar stage will usually zero in on concrete facts, but will not be able to analyze those facts or pull out abstract concepts. This is why the Baltimore Catechism is so effective with young children. They memorize the questions and answers of our Catholic faith and this builds a foundation for later stages when they're ready for deeper study. Much like children memorize their ABC's before learning to read and analyze books.

The grammar stage is a good time to learn Latin grammar with its unchanging, basic rules. The study of mathematics presents a perfect example of how the Trivium works. The grade (grammar) school student may excel at arithmetic (addition, subtraction, multiplication, and division), but will not have the analytical skills (Dialectic) for algebra or the abstract thinking skills (Rhetoric) for calculus. Similarly, reading selections for your grade school student should not require thinking skills beyond their grasp. Stick to basic stories.

To make history concrete, use a timeline or Book of Centuries, this gives the child a tangible view of historical events. Also useful at this stage are hands-on projects such as lapbooking, dioramas, and crafts. If you want to reinforce lessons learned by your grammar student, occasionally skip the book report and get creative.

Finally, take advantage of memorization skills and give your grammar students poems, or passages from a favorite book, to recite from memory. This gets them used to hearing, and speaking, good language. In my homeschool support group, we have a popular club call Book Buddies. Homeschooled children gather together once a month to recite memorized poems and give book reports. It's fun for the children, encourages them in their schoolwork, and gives them an opportunity to practice public speaking skills.

Dialectic (Logic)

When I think of the Dialectic Stage, I think of my lawyer-minded middle school students. Immediate obedience is sidelined as they question my every request. This is the stage where students will want to explore the "why" of everything. Their books will move from basic stories to more complicated plotlines.

Now is the time to move from arts and crafts to creative writing projects. Give them good books to read and then discuss them in a logical manner. Have your student support opinions about their books and lessons with facts and truth, rather than just strong feelings. They should be able to compare the heroes and villains of their stories, pulling out the character traits that separate them.

Mortimer Adler's book *How to Read a Book: The Art of Getting a Liberal Education* sets down *rules* for finding understanding from books, which I think can be used by a student in the Dialectic (Logic) stage. In order to truly learn we need to *understand*, not just remember more information. For example, when a writer is sharing something above our student's head, we can show them how to rise to understand what it is the writer is trying to communicate. One rule Adler gives is to pick out and interpret the important or most-repeated words in a book. Then discover the important sentences. If the words in a sentence have more than one meaning, analyze the sentence and decide the author's intent.

Adler also states that reading shouldn't be a passive activity. Have your student ask the book questions. Of course books aren't alive and cannot answer, so the student will need to find the answers himself. For example: In Chesterton's poem *The Donkey*, what does he mean by "When fishes flew?" When were "palms laid before [the donkey's] feet?"

It would be easy to search out commentaries on

books in order to find others' opinions, but we wouldn't learn anything of significance. We would only learn of other's opinions, rather than truly understanding the book. Don't analyze books for your student. Instead encourage him to find meaning and understanding for himself, by using the steps mentioned here.

Rhetoric

When students reach high school they have mastered the tools of memorizing facts and of analyzing those facts. They are now ready to engage in the art of expression and in the science of communication. This is not the time to let one's child go, but to continue helping him flower, guiding him gently. Challenge his thinking skills during this stage and make him defend his intellectual and religious positions.

Introduce Socratic discussion at this phase. Engage your high school student in conversation about their books. Asking probing questions will help them make connections, come up with insightful conclusions, and retain lessons learned. This is what is known as the Socratic method, named after the Greek philosopher. Socrates didn't leave behind any great writings. What we know of him, comes from his students, Plato, Aristotle, and Xenophon. Socrates didn't teach through lecture, but through question-

🖳 **Helpful Websites**

www.thomasaquinas.edu/curriculum/socratic.htm
The Socratic method. From Thomas Aquinas College (TAC)
www-ed.fnal.gov/trc/tutorial/taxonomy.html
Taxonomy of Socratic questions
www.newadvent.org/cathen/14119a.htm
Biography of Socrates

ing. He approached his students as though he were igno-rant, and then asked specific questions about a subject until the students had to confess their own ignorance. At this

📖 **Further Reading**

Designing Your Own Classical Curriculum by Laura Berquist
Lost Tools of Learning by Dorothy Sayers – Can be pur-chased from Emmanuel Books (see appendix) or as a free download by searching the Internet.

point, Socrates would start asking questions that would bring up a new way to view the subject, thus opening the students' eyes to new ideas and aspects.

During the Rhetoric stage, you can move from nar-rative stories to challenging critiques and debates. Go beyond your textbook and explore primary documents, such as autobiographies, docu-ments, letters, and speeches. Give the high school student an opportunity to see how the turns of history occurred through first-hand accounts.

🖉 **Cool Quote**

From Dorothy Sayers' "Lost Tools of Learning": "The doors of the store-house of knowledge should now be thrown open for them to browse about as they will. The things once learned by rote will be seen in new contexts."

High school is the per-fect time to teach apologetics. Teach him to apply his Baltimore Catechism and Bible facts to reasoned debate. Study the Early Church Fathers, how their leadership formed the way we worship today, and how the books of the Bible were determined.

Look for the historical and biblical perspectives in studying science. Study the ethical ramifications in scien-tific research. Relevant topics for today may include stem cell research, fetal tissue transplants, and cloning.

In the end, you want a student who is a good rhetorician, not a debater. His goal should not be to win arguments, but to get to the core of issues raised, to find Truth.

📖 **Further Reading**

Socrates Meets Jesus by Peter Kreeft
Philosophy 101 by Socrates by Peter Kreeft
Socratic Circles: Fostering Critical and Creative Thinking in Middle and High School by Matt Copeland
Socrates Café by Christopher Phillips

Classical Education

Charlotte Mason

Charlotte Mason was a nineteenth century educator in England and her educational philosophy is very popular with twenty-first century homeschoolers. She promoted the training of habits and short lessons. Her method of education included the use of *living* or *real* books, narration, dictation, copywork, Book of Centuries, journaling, and nature studies

Though Charlotte Mason was not a Catholic, her educational philosophy is easily baptized. Some of her ideas are borrowed from the classical education model, which is Catholic. Narration, dictation, and copywork all train the mind and work well with children in the grammar stage. Nature studies develop a love for the world created by God. And it goes without saying that the training of habits is a good thing. Most appealing about a Charlotte Mason education is the respect given to children as unique gifts from God with the ability to reason and love.

> ✐ **Cool Quote**
>
> "From their earliest days, they should get the habit of reading literature which they should take hold of for themselves, much or little, in their own way"
> Charlotte Mason
> [*Philosophy of Education*, Volume 6, Original Homeschooling Series, pg. 191]

Living Books

If you find yourself in a room filled with Charlotte Mason (CM) enthusiasts, it won't be long before you hear them speaking about *twaddle*. "Twaddle" is as near a derogatory word as you can get in CM circles. Twaddle is the opposite of a living book. Twaddle can also be applied to educational activities. It means to be dumbed-down, or simply a waste of time. Some might describe twaddle as "eye candy" or even "brain candy." It's a fleeting pleasure, but with little to no substantial or lasting meaningful themes.

Generally speaking, textbooks and fill-in-the-blanks workbooks (there are always exceptions of course) are categorized as twaddle because they're usually formulaic rather than thought provoking. They take the life out of the story and bring it down to the bare bones, the bare facts.

Living books on the other hand are just that – living. They awaken a child's imagination through their God-given curiosity, and sense of wonder, in a manner that is savored and enjoyed. Living books are not condescending in their tone and take education out of the classroom, making it a part of everyday life.

Narration

The first year I homeschooled, I followed Laura Berquist's advice in *Designing Your Own Classical Curriculum* and used narration in teaching my young children Bible history. I would read a Bible story to them and they would then retell the story to me in their own words and draw a corresponding picture in their art sketchbooks. I continued to use this method in the proceeding years. The idea was to make sure my children understood the pivotal points of the story. Also, by verbalizing what they hear, children are using multiple senses to retain lessons learned through the story.

When one of my children required speech therapy, she was extensively tested to make sure there weren't other developmental issues. She scored off the charts for reading comprehension. The teacher who administered the test was amazed this child could not only retell a story, but could also recall the smallest detail. When I told the teacher of our narration lessons, she said it was the reason for my child's extraordinary performance. Narration was something I did just three days a week for a short period of time, yet it produced outstanding results.

Dictation

A short written piece is read out loud to the child, who then writes it word for word on his paper. He should attempt to use proper spelling and punctuation. I find the DK Eyewitness books are good for this exercise. They provide little factual snippets, which my younger children love. I simply choose a sentence or more (depending on the child's development), read it aloud slowly, and wait for the child to write it in their notebook. We then go over the written work together, with me gently making corrections. It's a very short, yet easy, exercise to implement. It teaches the habit of paying attention, as well as sentence structure, punctuation, spelling, and so on.

Copywork

Copywork is similar to dictation. However, instead of the text being verbally dictated it is silently read by the student. Give a child a paragraph from a favorite book and have them copy it directly from the book. Then check it for penmanship, punctuation, capitalization, etc. This helps develop an eye for good writing. It also helps develop the habit of being detail-oriented. The child will learn to pay close attention to the minute details that make up a story, as well as develop an appreciation for the beauty and grace found in a well-told story.

Book of Centuries

Charlotte Mason had her students keep a Book of Centuries. This is basically an historical timeline kept in a notebook or three-ring binder. The child writes about an historical event on each page. You could also include titles of books read, pictures, names, dates, and so on.

I like to use a three-ring binder so pages can be easily moved or inserted. This keeps the pages in our Book of Centuries in chronological order. Another idea is to put your Book of Centuries' pages into three-hole punched, plastic sheet protectors.

Journaling

Charlotte Mason would give her students, aged ten and up, free time each week to write whatever pleased them in their journals. While dictation and copywork are corrected by the teacher, journals are meant to be free expression. In my homeschool, I combine journaling with nature studies. The children journal about discoveries found in our woods – animals, plants, tracks, and so on.

Nature Study

Though Charlotte Mason loved order, she gave her students plenty of time for free play. She put a lot of importance on getting children into the out-of-doors. She wrote, "He must live hours daily in the open air . . . must look and touch and listen; must be quick to note, consciously, every peculiarity of habit or structure, in beast, bird, or insect; the manner of growth and fructification of every plant. He must be accustomed to ask why – Why does the wind blow? Why does the river flow? Why is a leaf-bud sticky? And do not hurry to answer his question for him; let him think his difficulties out so far as his small experience will carry him."

When the weather is pleasant, you'll likely find one or more of my children reading books in the backyard. When they're not reading you'll find them playing or exploring, even when the weather is quite unpleasant. These two things are important to a child's complete education, perhaps as much as their book work.

To explore is to learn to observe and make

"He must live hours daily in the open air . . . must look and touch and listen; must be quick to note, consciously, every peculiarity of habit or structure, in beast, bird, or insect; the manner of growth and fructification of every plant. He must be accustomed to ask why–Why does the wind blow? Why does the river flow? Why is a leaf-bud sticky? And do not hurry to answer his question for him; let him think his difficulties out so far as his small experience will carry him."-Charlotte Mason [*Nocturnal Philosophy: The Basic Facts*, Vol I, Original Homeschooling Series, pg 265]

hypotheses about the world God created for them. It helps create a sense of wonder, a sense of awe. Free play, not organized play but spontaneous play, promotes creativity, discovery, and inter-personal relationships.

All of these Charlotte Mason techniques lend themselves well to the use of real books. You can choose great literature for narration, dictation, or copywork. You can find interesting books to accompany discoveries made in nature studies. Lessons learned in reading historical fiction or biographies can be transferred to a Book of Centuries. Journal entries can be made about favorite books. Yes, a Charlotte Mason education can be implemented in teaching core subjects with literature.

📖 Further Reading

To learn more, check out these Charlotte Mason books:
Real Learning: Education in the Heart of the Home by Elizabeth Foss [By Way of the Family]
A Charlotte Mason Companion: Personal Reflections on the Gentle Art of Learning by Karen Andreola
For the Children's Sake by Susan S. MacAulay
The Original Homeschooling Series by Charlotte Mason
When Children Love to Learn: A Practical Application of Charlotte Mason's Philosophy for Today by Elaine Cooper

Also check out:
Education in the Out of Doors by MacBeth Derham [*The Catholic Homeschool Companion*, Sophia Institute Press, 2005, pg. 169-173]

How to Create a Literature Unit Study

This is not a book about unit studies. However, I suspect a number of readers would like to be able to create unit studies around the books found in the literary guides.

If you are unfamiliar with unit studies, they are theme-based studies that incorporate many academic disciplines. For example, if you're studying the Renaissance you might gather books about the great artists, composers, scientists, and mathematicians of the era. You would of course include the religious upheaval of the day and perhaps even incorporate apologetics into your unit. For a truly complete unit study, you could cook up authentic recipes, draw political maps or build a relief map, and learn about the currency and economics. You would find related words for spelling and vocabulary. Perhaps visit a museum with Renaissance art, learn about the dress of the day (for both the aristocrats and the paupers), and check out videos that take place during the period such as *A Man for All Seasons* or *The Reluctant Saint*.

Here's a checklist to help you get started in creating your own unit studies:

☐ Decide on a topic or historical era.
☐ Choose books.
  ☐ Fictional literature set in era being studied.
  ☐ Biographies and autobiographies.
  ☐ Non-fiction books, core subjects: music, art, math, science, and history.
  ☐ Non-fiction books, non-core subjects: geography, philosophy, political science, etc.
  ☐ Religious.
    ☐ Saints.
    ☐ Bible verses for memorization.
    ☐ Catechism of the Catholic Church.

- ☐ Language arts.
    - ☐ Writing assignments.
        - ☐ Book reports.
        - ☐ Journal.
        - ☐ Creative writing.
        - ☐ Dictation.
        - ☐ Vocabulary and spelling words.
        - ☐ Note taking.
- ☐ Arts and crafts.
    - ☐ Dioramas.
    - ☐ Lapbooks.
    - ☐ Scrapbooks.
    - ☐ Mobiles.
    - ☐ Posters.
    - ☐ Sculptures.
    - ☐ Relief maps.
- ☐ Science projects and experiments.
- ☐ Drama.
    - ☐ Create a one-act play, puppet show, newscast, etc.
    - ☐ Make costumes and set.
- ☐ Timeline or Book of Centuries.
- ☐ Videos.
- ☐ Family connections.
- ☐ Check for Internet resources.
    - ☐ Free unit studies on same or related topic.
    - ☐ Outline maps.
    - ☐ Period or ethnic recipes.
- ☐ Field trip opportunities.
    - ☐ Museums.
    - ☐ Zoos.
    - ☐ Ethnic or period restaurants.
    - ☐ Ethnic neighborhoods.
    - ☐ Factories.
- ☐ Other.

This is an extensive list. You don't need to check off every box. Pick and choose what works for you and your homeschool. If you have no interest in cooking period food or using the Internet, then don't. Factor in the amount of time you can comfortably set aside for your unit, the interests of your children, and your easy access to resources.

> 📖 **Further Reading**
>
> **Resources for creating your own unit study:**
> Integrated Learning or Unit Studies: Design-Your-Own or Ready-Made? by Pattie Kelley-Huff [*The Catholic Homeschool Companion*, Sophia Institute Press, 2005, pg. 175-183]
> *Unit Studies 101* by Amanda Bennett

Ready-made unit studies for purchase:
ABC's of Christian Culture by Julia Fogassy [Our Father's House]
Connecting with History: A Catholic Guide to History by Sonya Romens [RCHistory]
History Links [Wooly Lamb]

Heart and Mind – A quarterly Catholic homeschooling magazine, which has a pull-out unit study in every issue. Most are literature based. (*Heart and Mind* also has a regular literature column.) www.heart-and-mind.com or PO Box 420881, San Diego, CA 92142

> 💻 **Helpful Website**
>
> See www.maureen-wittmann.com for free downloadable forms to help you create your own unit study, as well as a few ready-made units.

Literary Guides

Art and Music Appreciation

There are many beautiful art and music appreciation books available. So many that these subjects can be
pure joy to share with children. There isn't much in this literary guide that will assist you directly in practical art or
music instruction; however, children will be more open to
picking up a brush or an instrument if they have first
developed an appreciation. Much like we read aloud to
children long before we teach them phonics, so go the arts.

The first year I homeschooled, the children and I did
an in-depth study of the great composers. Each week, I
read a biography of a composer aloud to my children while
listening to his music. We checked out both the books and
the recordings from the library. It was a very good experience for us all.

Years later, we did a similar study with the great
artists. I displayed works of art as I read a biography of the
artist to the children. I easily found famous paintings on
the Internet and saved them as my computer wallpaper. I
also printed several, putting them into frames or making
them into homemade magnets. It's also easy to find inexpensive art posters at art galleries and museums.

As you read the following books with your children, I
encourage you to listen to the corresponding music or dis-
play the corresponding art. This simple exercise will greatly enrich your lessons.

Overview
*The Annotated Mona Lisa: A Crash Course in Art
    History from Prehistoric to Post-Modern* by Carol

Strickland – An easy-to-read reference book for teachers and parents. Could be taken along on trips to the art museum.

A

Art in Story: Teaching Art History to Elementary School Children by Marianne Saccardi – A wonderful resource for facilitating a personal connection between art, artist, and student. Its strength lies in personal stories for nearly every art period and artist. You'll find ideas for journaling, drama, art projects, and more. Written for teachers and librarians working with children grades 3-8.

A

Teaching Art With Books Kids Love: Teaching Art Appreciation, Elements of Art, and Principles of Design With Award-Winning Children's Books by Darcie Clark Frohardt – Written for the teachers of grades 3-5. Especially good for learning technical terms. One comes to appreciate various art periods and what distinguishes them, but not until you've had a chance to understand value, color, space, harmony, contrast, balance, texture, movement, and dominance.

A

Classical Music for Dummies by David Pogue and Scott Speck – I hesitate recommending a "Dummies" book. However, if you don't mind the irreverent tone, this is actually a fairly good guide. Comes with a CD of sample tracks.

H, A

Classical Music 101: A Complete Guide to Learning and Loving Classical Music by Fred Plotkin – A basic introduction to Western classical music. Interspersed with interviews with classical musicians. Could be used as a music textbook.

H, A

Art and Music Appreciation

Homegrown Music: Discovering Bluegrass by Stephanie P. Ledgin – Learn a little Americana as you explore the history of bluegrass music.
H, A

In Tiers of Glory: The Organic Development of Catholic Church Architecture Through the Ages by Michael S. Rose [Mesa Folio] – Written for the layman, examines the historical aspects of the Catholic tradition in church architecture.
H, A, ✠

The Inner Game of Music by Barry Green with W. Timothy Gallwey – Written for musicians. Like a coach in a book (based on *The Inner Game of Tennis*), teaches readers how to overcome the jitters, concentrate better, and improve skills. Could be used by parents and teachers to help their students.
H, A

Jazz 101: A Complete Guide to Learning and Loving Jazz by John F. Szwed – The author is both an anthropologist and a music scholar. He gives the reader all the key figures, history, theory, and controversies that shaped jazz's development. There is also a list of the most important recordings.
H, A

The NPR Curious Listener's Guide Series – I like the easy-to-read format of this inexpensive series. Gives brief descriptions of major musical works and profiles of composers and musicians. Information is organized alphabetically rather than chronologically, so it can be confusing if you are tying the book into music history.
The NPR Curious Listener's Guide to Jazz by Loren Schoenberg
The NPR Curious Listener's Guide to American Folk Music by Kip Lornell

The NPR Curious Listener's Guide to Blues by David Evans

The NPR Curious Listener's Guide to Celtic Music by Fioni Ritchie

The NPR Curious Listener's Guide to Classical Music by Tim Smith

The NPR Curious Listener's Guide to Opera by William Berger

The NPR Curious Listener's Guide to Popular Standards by Max Morath

The NPR Curious Listener's Guide to World Music by Chris Nickson

H, A

The NPR Guide to Building a Classical CD Collection: The 350 Essential Works by Ted Libbey – This is the guide to own if you would like to expand your knowledge, and your CD collection, in the area of classical music. Informative and easy to digest.

H, A

Opera 101: A Complete Guide to Learning and Loving Opera by Fred Plotkin – A brief history of opera, plus a detailed analysis of eleven key operas.

H, A

Sister Wendy's Story of Painting by Sister Wendy Beckett [DK] (second edition) – Sister Wendy's vivid, personal interpretations of nearly 450 paintings. Awesome collection, but you may want to use discretion as great art often depicts nudity. If you like this book, check out Sister Wendy's other titles and videos.

H, A, ✠, *

Stopping Time: The Photographs of Harold Edgerton by Gus Kayafas and Estelle Jussim – Harold Edgerton was the inventor of strobe flash and pioneer of stop-action photography. Photography is also art and a

great discipline for older students to study.
H, A

The Vintage Guide to Classical Music by Jan Swafford –
Possibly the best guide available. Chronologically
arranged from Gregorian Chant to Baroque to Modern.
Includes a glossary of musical terms and help in build-
ing a classical music library.
H, A

What to Listen for in Music by Aaron Copland –
Originally published in 1957, Copland's guide to
music is a little outdated but still a valuable read for
both the novice and the virtuoso.
H, A

***Who's Afraid of Classical Music: A Highly Arbitrary and
Thoroughly Opinionated Guide to Listening to and
Enjoying Symphony, Opera and Chamber Music*** by
Michael Walsh – A bit of an unconventional, yet very
good, guide to classical music.
H, A

***Heavenly City: The Architectural Tradition of Catholic
Chicago*** by Denis R. McNamara [Liturgy Training] –
A well researched book that is also eye catching. Full-
color photographs and architectural descriptions of
Chicago's most beautiful Catholic churches and
chapels.
M, H, A, ✠

***In the Footsteps of Popes: A Spirited Guide to the
Treasures of the Vatican*** by Enrico Bruschini
[William Morrow] – The author is an art historian and
former curator of fine art at the American Embassy in
Rome. This book is like going on a personal tour of
Vatican City.
M, H, A, ✠

Rome: Art & Architecture by Marco Bussagli, editor
[Konemann] – Beautiful photographs detailing Rome's

artistic and architectural treasures. Moves chronologically through history in its detail.

M, H, A, ✠

Art Through Faith by Mary Lynch and Seton Staff [Seton Educational Media] – This book is meant to be used as an eighth grade textbook, however I've shared it with children of all ages with great success.

G, M, H, ✠

Sing Me a Story: The Metropolitan Opera's Book of Opera Stories for Children by Jane Rosenberg, introduction by Luciano Pavarotti – Nicely illustrated collection of fifteen opera stories. Presented to children in an enjoyable way, from *The Barber of Seville* to *Aida*.

M

DK Read & Listen: Illustrated Book of Ballet Stories by Barbara Newmann – A nice introduction to ballet. Tells the stories of *Sleeping Beauty*, *Giselle*, *Coppelia*, *Swan Lake*, and *The Nutcracker.* Includes illustrations from the ballets.

G, M

Of Swans, Sugarplums, and Satin Slippers: Ballet Stories for Children by Violette Verdy, illustrated by Marcia Brown – The stories of six of the best-loved ballets: *The Firebird*, *Coppilia*, *Swan Lake*, *The Nutcracker*, *Giselle*, and *Sleeping Beauty*, recounted by a former principal ballerina with the New York City Ballet. She gives careful explanations of the dancers' movements, making this an excellent source for anyone seeing the ballets in person, on video, or DVD.

G, M

The World's Very Best Opera for Kids . . . in English! – This audio CD is a great way to introduce children to opera. You'll enjoy listening too.

G, M

Art Fraud Detective: Spot the Difference, Solve the Crime! by Anna Nilsen – Depicts various works of art in a fictitious museum, most of which are frauds. Also contains depictions of the real paintings, so they can be compared by the reader to determine the frauds.
G

The Barefoot Book of Stories from the Opera by Shahrukh Husain and James Mayhew – Colorful book providing children with the story lines of seven operas: Britten's *The Little Sweep*, Mozart's *The Magic Flute*, Humperdinck's *Hansel and Gretel*, Wagner's *The Flying Dutchman*, Rossini's *La Cenerentola*, Von Gluck's *Orpheus and Eurydice*, and Rimsky-Korsakov's *Christmas Eve*. Each retelling takes about 10 pages.
G

A Child's Book of Art: Great Pictures First Words by Lucy Micklethwait – Gorgeous introduction to art appreciation written for young children, but good for all ages.
P, G, M

A Child's Book of Prayer in Art by Sister Wendy Beckett [DK] – Classic works of art that speak to children. Of particular interest to homeschoolers is the painting *The Young Schoolmistress*, where Sister Wendy notes: "Perhaps she is his big sister and he is being taught in his own at home. It is not only in the classroom, or from qualified teachers, that we learn about the world."
P, G, ✠

Ah, Music! by Aliki – A delightful introduction to music for very young children. Answers the question "What is music?" in easy-to-understand terms.
P, G

I Spy Series by Lucy Micklethwait – Combines the fun of playing "I Spy" with art appreciation.
I Spy Two Eyes: Numbers in Art
I Spy: An Alphabet in Art
I Spy A Lion: Animals in Art
I Spy a Freight Train: Transportation in Art
P

Historical Timeline
Moses (c. 1250 BC)
The Life of Moses **(Art Revelations)** by Neil Morris – This series is a wonderful way to study both Scripture and art. This volume contains 13 depictions of Moses by famous artists from Botticelli to Michelangelo.
M, H

The Life of Christ (c.0-33 AD)
The Life of Jesus **(Art Revelations)** by Neil Morris – Some of the history's greatest paintings depicting the Annunciation, Nativity, Baptism, Sermon on the Mount, Last Supper, Crucifixion, Resurrection and Ascension.
M, H

Emperor Justinian (518-565), Byzantine Icons
Brother Joseph: The Painter of Icons by Fr. Augustine DeNoble [Bethlehem] – A lovely story of a modern-day boy, encouraged by his grade-school teacher, who grows up to be a painter of icons. Beautifully illustrated.
G, ☩

Gregorian Chant (c. 600)

An Introduction to Gregorian Chant by Richard L.
Crocker – Read this as you listen to *Chant* by The
Benedictine Monks of Santo Domingo de Silos or
your favorite Gregorian Chant CD.
H, A

Byzantine (330-1453)
**Cimabue, formerly Benciviene di Pepo (c.1251-1302),
Italy**
Giotto di Bondone (c.1266-1337), Italy

The Glorious Impossible by Madeleine L'Engle – Uses
Giotto di Bondone's frescoes from the Scrovegni
Chapel to take the reader from the Annunciation
through the Pentecost. The pictures are awesome.
Note: The author mentions the Blessed Mother's pain
in childbirth. The Church teaches the birth of Jesus
was painless.
G, M

A Boy Named Giotto by Paolo Guarnieri, illustrated by
Bimba Landmann, translated by Jonathan Galassi –
Eight-year-old Giotto, then a shepherd boy, confesses
his dream of becoming an artist to famed painter
Cimabue, who takes him on as his pupil.
P, G

Art: Renaissance Period (c. 1400-1600)
Donatello (1386-1466), Italy
Giovanni Bellini (1428-1516), Italy
Sandro Botticelli (1445-1510), Italy
Leonardo da Vinci (1452-1519), Italy
Michelangelo Bounarroti (1475-1564), Italy
Raphael (1483-1520), Italy
Pieter Bruegel (1525-1569), Netherlands

Notebooks of Leonardo da Vinci – Go straight to the source. Leonardo's diary in his own handwriting (with translations) and sketches.
H, A

The Second Mrs. Gioconda by E. L. Konigsburg – This historical fiction tells a story of why Leonardo da Vinci took three years to finish the Mona Lisa, all while great monarchs were begging to have their portraits painted. My middle school daughter loved this book.
M, H

First Impressions Series – This series is written by several authors. Great to use in tying together history and art.
First Impressions: Leonardo Da Vinci by Richard McLanathan
First Impressions: Michelangelo by Richard McLanathan
M, H, A

Leonardo Da Vinci by Diane Stanley – I love Stanley's old world style illustrations. DaVinci is fascinating to study.
.   M

Michelangelo by Diane Stanley – Goes into the details of Michelangelo's work, including his dissecting of human cadavers.
M

Leonardo da Vinci for Kids: His Life and Ideas, 21
Activities **(For Kids Series)** by Janis Herbert – An
historical biography plus projects.
G, M

What Makes a Leonardo a Leonardo? by Richard
Muhlberger – This is a favorite series. It really brings
an appreciation for art. Written for the 9 to 12 set, it's
worthwhile for older students too.
G, M

What Makes a Raphael a Raphael? by Richard
Muhlberger
G, M

What Makes a Bruegel a Bruegel? by Richard
Muhlberger
G, M

Getting to Know the World's Greatest Artists Series by
Mike Venezia – These are some of my favorite books
for children. Venezia's cartoons, combined with repro-
ductions of great works of art, invite children into the
world of art appreciation.
Botticellli
Da Vinci
Michelangelo
Raphael
Peter Bruegel
P, G

Leonardo and the Flying Boy: A Story about Leonardo
Da Vinci by Laurence Anholt – Takes two real characters from da Vinci's life, Zoro and Salai, and creates a
fun story that demonstrates Da Vinci's fascination with
flying machines.
P, G

Music: Renaissance Period (c. 1400-1600)
Giovanni Palestrina (c. 1525-1594), Italy

Art: Baroque Period (c. 1600-1750)
Giovanni Lorenzo Bernini (1598-1680), Italy
Diego Velasquez (1599-1660), Spain
Rembrandt van Rijn (1606-1669), Netherlands
I, Juan de Pareja by Elizabeth de Trevino – Juan is Diego
  Velasquez's slave and personal assistant. Juan's story
  is beautiful and centers on his Catholic faith. A must
  read.
  M, H, ✠
First Impressions: Rembrandt by Gary Schwartz
  M, H, A
What Makes a Rembrandt a Rembrandt? by Richard
  Muhlberger
  M, H
Rembrandt **(Getting to Know the World's Greatest**
  Artists Series) by Mike Venezia
  P, G

Music: Baroque Period (c. 1600-1750)
Claudio Monteverdi (1567-1643), Italy and Austria
Antonio Vivaldi (1678-1741), Italy
Johann Sebastian Bach (1685-1750), Germany
George Frideric Handel (1685-1759), Germany and
  England
Music Masters Series – Audio biographies. These tapes
  and CD's tell the stories of the great composers,
  alongside several selections of their greatest composi-
  tions.
  The Story of Vivaldi & Corelli
  The Story of Bach
  The Story of Handel
  G, M

Art and Music Appreciation

Classical Kids Series – Audio dramas. My children love
this series. I collected them one by one, putting them
into the children's stockings at Christmas.
Vivaldi's Ring of Mystery
Mr. Bach Comes to Call
Hallelujah Handel
G, M

Famous Children Series by Ann Rachlin – This series
recounts events from the childhoods of famous com-
posers.
Bach
Handel
G

**Getting to Know the World's Greatest Composers
Series** by Mike Venezia – Venezia's series on the great
composers is just as good as his series on the great
artists. The children laugh at his funny cartoons, which
helps them remember the stories.
Johann Sebastian Bach
George Handel
P, G

Art: Classical Period (c. 1750-1825)
Benjamin West (1738-1820), U. S. and England
Francisco Goya (1746-1828), France
First Impressions: Francisco Goya by Ann Waldron
M, H, A
What Makes a Goya a Goya? by Richard Muhlberger
G, M
The Boy Who Loved to Draw: Benjamin West by Barbara
Brenner – Known by some as the "Father of American
Art," West was the tenth child born of his family. His
childhood story is inspirational.
G

Art and Music Appreciation

Music: Classical Period (c. 1750-1825)
Franz Joseph Haydn (1732-1809), Austria
Wolfgang Amadeus Mozart (1756-1791), Austria
Ludwig van Beethoven (1770-1827), Germany and
Austria

Music Masters Series – Audio biographies.
The Story of Haydn
The Story of Mozart
The Story of Beethoven
G, M

Classical Kids Series – Audio dramas.
Mozart's Magic Fantasy
Mozart's Magnificent Voyage
Beethoven Lives Upstairs
G, M

The Farewell Symphony by Anna Harwell Celenza, illustrated by JoAnn Kitchel – A memorable story about
Haydn's Symphony No. 45 *Farewell.* Includes a CD
of the symphony.
G

Famous Children Series by Ann Rachlin
Mozart
Beethoven
G

Getting to Know the World's Greatest Composers
Series by Mike Venezia
Wolfgang Amedeus
Ludwig Van Beethoven
P, G

Art: Romantic Period (c. 1815-1900)

Art: Impressionism (c.1867-1886)
Edouard Manet (1832-1883), France
Edgar Degas (1834-1917), Italy

Claude Monet (1840-1926), France
Pierre Auguste Renior (1841-1919), France
Mary Cassatt (1844-1926), United States and France
Vincent Van Gogh (1853-1890), Netherlands
First Impressions Series

> *First Impressions: Edgar Degas* by Susan E. Meyers
> *First Impressions: Monet* by Ann Waldron
> *First Impressions: Cassatt* by Susan E. Abrams
> M, H, A

Linnea in Monet's Garden by Christina Bjork and Lena Anderson – Linnea is a little girl with a love for art and flowers. She travels with her neighbor Mr. Bloom to France to see the estate of Claude Monet and the museums displaying his art. The book includes reproductions of Monet's paintings, old family photographs, and photographs of his estate.
G, M

What Makes a Monet a Monet? by Richard Muhlberger
G, M

What Makes a Degas a Degas? by Richard Muhlberger
G, M

What Makes a Cassatt a Cassatt? by Richard Muhlberger
G, M

What Makes a Van Gogh a Van Gogh? by Richard Muhlberger
G, M

Katie Meets the Impressionists by James Mayhew – Cute story of a little girl who visits a museum with her grandmother. She jumps into the paintings, looking for flowers for Grandmother and finds the Impressionists.
P, G

Degas and the Little Dancer: A Story About Edgar Degas by Laurence Anholt – The story of Marie, a French girl who dreams of the ballet and who models for

Degas. Children will remember the story whenever they see the *Little Dancer* sculpture.

P, G

Camille and the Sunflowers: A Story about Vincent VanGogh by Laurence Anholt – Like Anholt's other books, based on a real-life encounter between the artist and a child.

.   P, G

Getting to Know the World's Greatest Artists Series by Mike Venezia

Edgar Degas

Monet

Pierre Auguste Renoir

Mary Cassatt

Van Gogh

P, G

Music: Romantic Period (c. 1815-1900)

Franz Schubert (1797-1828), Austria

Hector Berlioz (1803-1869), France

Feliz Mendelssohn (1809-1847), Germany

Frederic Chopin (1810-1849), Poland

Franz Liszt (1811-1886), Hungary, France, and Italy

Guiseppe Verdi (1813-1901), Italy

Johannes Brahms (1833-1897), Germany

Peter Ilich Tchaikovsky (1840-1893), Russia

Music Masters Series – Audio biographies.

The Story of Schubert

The Story of Berlioz

The Story of Mendelssohn

The Story of Chopin

The Story of Verdi

The Story of Brahms

The Story of Tchaikovsky

G, M

Tchaikovsky Discovers America (**Classical Kids Series**) –
Audio drama.
G, M
Famous Children Series by Ann Rachlin
Schubert
Chopin
Brahms
Tchaikovsky
G
**Getting to Know the World's Greatest Composers
Series** by Mike Venezia
Frederick Chopin
Johannes Brahms
Peter Tchaikovsky
P, G

Art: Modern Period (c. 1900-1950)
Paul Cezanne (1839-1906), France
Pablo Picasso (1881-1973), Spain and France
Marc Chagall (1887-1985), Russia and France
Norman Rockwell (1894-1978), U.S.
Ansel Adams (1902-1984), U.S.
Salvadore Dali (1904-1989), Spain
Ansel Adams: An Autobiography – From Adam's child-
hood discovery of the High Sierras to his conservation
work with several U.S. presidents. Learn about his
technical and esthetic styles, as well as why his work
influences so many photographers still today.
H, A
First Impressions: Pablo Picasso by John Beardsley
M, H, A
What Makes a Picasso a Picasso? by Richard Muhlberger
G, M
Getting to Know the World's Greatest Artists Series
Paul Cezanne

Picasso
Marc Chagal
Norman Rockwell
Salvadore Dali
P, G

Picasso and the Girl with a Ponytail by Laurence Anholt
 – An adorable, and true, story about a young girl who
 is taken under the wing of an elderly Picasso.
 P, G

Music: Modern Period (c. 1900-1950)
John Philip Sousa (1845-1932). U.S.
George Gershwin (1898-1937), U.S.
Igor Stravinsky (1882-1971), Russia
Duke Ellington (1899-1974), U.S.
Aaron Copland (1900-1990), U.S.

The Story of Foster & Sousa **(Music Masters Series)** –
 Audio biography.
 G, M

Duke Ellington: The Piano Prince and His Orchestra by
 Andrea and Brian Pinkney – As a child, Duke wanted
 to play baseball rather than practice his piano lessons.
 An appreciation of music that developed in his teens
 brought him back to the piano.
 G

**Getting to Know the World's Greatest Composers
Series** by Mike Venezia
 John Philip Sousa
 George Gershwin
 Igor Stravinsky
 Duke Ellington
 Aaron Copland
 P, G

Music: American Jazz
Thelonious Monk (1917-1982), U.S.
Ella Fitzgerald (1917-1996), U.S.
Charlie Parker (1920-1955), U.S.
John (William) Coltrane (1926-1967), U.S.
The First Book of Jazz by Langston Hughes   -
    Written in 1955, this introduction covers the historical
    development of jazz.
    G

Ella Fitzgerald: The Tale of a Vocal Virtuosa by Andrea
    and Brian Pinkney – Ella's first dream was to be a
    dancer, however when nerves overcame her first dance
    performance at the famed Apollo Theatre, she sang
    instead. The rest is history.
    G

John Coltrane's Giant Steps by Chris Raschka –
    Coltrane's musical composition is performed by a box,
    a snowflake, some raindrops, and a kitten.
    G

Mysterious Thelonious by Chris Raschka – Matches the
    tones of the diatonic scale to the values of the color
    wheel in presenting a portrait of Thelonious Monk's
    work.
    G

Charlie Parker Played Be Bop by Chris Raschka –
    Introduces the famous saxophonist and his style of
    jazz known as be bop.
    G

Jazzy Alphabet by Sherry Shahan, illustrated by Mary
    Thelen – Introduce both jazz and the alphabet with
    this fun picture book.
    P

Art and Music Appreciation

Art and Music Appreciation

Math

My major in college was applied mathematics; yet, it was not until I became a homeschooling mother that I discovered math in literature. I find it a shame that few math teachers ever say "Hey let's take a break from this drill, drill, drill to enjoy reading *The Man Who Counted* aloud" or "Kids, we're going to read an interesting biography of a different mathematician each week" or "Let's work on our fun puzzle books for five minutes at the beginning of each class." No wonder children in this country have math phobia. It's almost as though there is a conspiracy to make math as dry and dull as possible so children absolutely hate it.

I don't think I would be far off the mark if I estimated seventy-five percent or more of the parents reading this book have said to their children, "Math was my worst subject in school" or worse, "I hate math!" I challenge every one of you to bite your tongue in the future, no matter how true the words may be. I encourage you instead to take a little break from the daily drill, and read aloud an interesting piece of literature showing mathematics in a glowing light.

Emotions are contagious. If your fear of math is clearly evident to your children, they will take on the same fear. If, on the other hand, you make a conscious decision to discover the beauty in math yourself, your children will greatly benefit and you will see a significant increase in their mathematical skills.

Yes, there is beauty in math. Just as God is orderly, so is math. There is beauty to be found in its orderliness and exactness. Reading about how the great proofs came to be or how mathematical discoveries were made can be very interesting. Many of the great mathematicians led colorful lives and reading their biographies may spark an interest in math, either in you or your child.

Think of it as math appreciation. We study music and art appreciation, and we should do the same with math (and other subjects, such as science for that matter). Imagine learning to play the piano without having first listened to music beautifully played by a professional. Imagine taking a painting class without having ever set eyes on the great works of the masters. It would take the joy out of learning. It would give you little which to aspire. Now, apply this thought to math. Use this math literary guide to find books that will help you and your children come to appreciate the great works of math.

At first finding math literature was quite a difficult task in putting together a reading list for my children. There are few resources available in this area. Adding to the difficulty was the task of weeding out books with anti-Catholic bias or salacious material. Yes, even math books contain trash.

✎ Cool Quote

"Insisting a child must be taught traditional, scope-and-sequence arithmetic to learn mathematics is like saying one must learn classical note and scales before one can learn music. You might get there, but you miss out on the inspiration of beautiful music created by the masters along the way.

We need not master all the 'basics' before being able to experience the appreciation that carries us through the hard work of learning. Think of applying living math principles as developing a 'mathematical ear' while working toward the mastery of basic theory." -Julie Brennan at www.livingmath.com.

I've spent countless hours searching the library, inter-library loan options, and the Internet for good math literature. This literary guide will, hopefully, save you from going through the same trouble.

> ⌨ **Helpful Websites**
>
> If you would like to discover even more math literature, check out http://charlottemason.tripod.com (MacBeth's Opinion) and www.livingmath.net (Living Math).

Overview

Math: Facing an American Phobia by Marilyn Burns – Written for math teachers, shows ways we can take the dread out of math. I got a lot out of this book.
A

Math Power: How to Help Your Child Love Math, Even if You Don't by Patricia Clark Kenschaft – Lots of ideas for teaching math and making it interesting for your student.
A

Vision in Elementary Mathematics by W. W. Sawyer – Helpful to teachers and parents in understanding the fundamentals of mathematics. Could be given to a high school student.
A

The Book of Numbers by John Conway and Richard Guy – A simplification of number theory. Includes color pictures and diagrams. Would be a nice accompaniment to a basic calculus course.
H, A

e: The Story of a Number by Eli Maor – Learn why e is one of the fundamental numbers. Explains difficult concepts with ease.
H, A

Gödel, Escher, Bach: An Eternal Golden Braid by
   Douglas Hofstadter – This is hefty volume explores
   the connection between the mathematics of Godel, the
   artwork of Escher, and the music of Bach. Written in
   1979, some parts about computers are dated.
   H, A

*The Golden Ratio: The Story of Phi, the World's Most
   Astonishing Number* by Mario Livio – Learn about
   phi, pi's under appreciated cousin.
   H, A

A History of Mathematics by Carl B. Boyer – The development of mathematics from ancient history to modern times, covering most of the important mathematicians and their discoveries.
   H, A

How to Solve It by George Polya – This is a classic on
   problem solving.
   H, A

*An Imaginary Tale: The Story of "i" [the square root of
   negative one]* by Paul Nahim – Learn about the number i, aka the square root of negative one. This title
   would be good for a high school senior who has at
   least completed pre-calculus.
   H, A

*Journey Through Genius: The Great Theorems of
   Mathematics* by William Dunham – History of the
   great proofs and the mathematics behind them.
   H, A

The Joy of Pi by David Blatner – Small, interesting, and
   easy-to-read.
   H, A

*The Lady Tasting Tea: How Statistics Revolutionized
   Science in the Twentieth Century* by David Salsburg
   – Starts with an experiment: Does tea taste different if
   the milk is poured into the tea instead of the tea

poured into the milk? Studies the lives of more than twenty statisticians. Could also be tied into science.
H, A

Mathematical Apocrypha: Stories and Anecdotes of Mathematicians and the Mathematical by Steven G. Krantz – Brief, some very brief, anecdotes about the lives of mathematicians. Arranged under sections devoted to great foolishness, great ideas, great failures, great pranks, and great people.
H, A, *

The Mathematical Experience by Philip Davis and Reuben Hersh – A collection of articles about mathematical philosophies, history, and biographies. This engaging read is also available in a study edition.
H, A

Mathematics and the Imagination by Edward Kasner – The study of mathematics does take an incredible amount of imagination. Considered a classic, this was written in 1940 by the man who coined the word *googol*. Great for high school.
H, A

The Mathematic Universe: An Alphabetical Journey Through the Great Proofs, and Personalities – An ABC book for grownups. Short essays to be read independently, hitting on a variety of topics.
H, A

The Number Sense: How the Mind Creates Mathematics by Stanislas Dehaene – Also a good book for science. Explores brain function in the area of mathematics.
H, A

Of Men and Numbers: The Story of the Great Mathematicians by Jane Muir – Compilation of biographies of great mathematicians.
H, A

Math

Wooden Book Series – Written by a variety of authors, these little books are fun, packed full of information, and inexpensive. Great for teenagers.

Harmonograph: A Visual Guide to Mathematics of Music by Anthony Ashton – This book is not only for the math student, but the music and art student as well.

Li: Dynamic Form in Nature by David Wade – Looking for patterns in nature is an awesome way to approach mathematics.

Platonic & Archimedean Solids by David Sutton – Explores the three-dimensional world. Give this to the student who loves design or architecture.

Sacred Geometry by Miranda Lundy – Explores the two-dimensional world and the influence of plane geometry in the Ancient world. Fun.

Stonehenge by Robin Heath – Analyzes the mysteries of the building of Stonehenge 5,000 years ago. Tie into your Ancient history studies.

Useful Mathematical and Physical Formulae by Matthew Watkins – I picked up this book at a used book sale for only a dollar. It turned out to be a great book to have on my reference shelf. A collection of commonly used math formulas. Also includes simple explanations of the laws of gravity and refraction.
H, A

Algebra Survival Guide: A Conversational Guide for the Thoroughly Befuddled by Josh Rappaport – Helps to make algebra understandable. Exercises (with answers) included. I would skip the accompanying workbook.
H

Algebra Unplugged by Ken Amdahl and Jim Loats, Ph.D. – My fifteen-year old used this alongside his formal algebra studies. Explains algebraic vocabulary, concepts, and strategies.

H

Calculus for Cats by Ken Amdahl and Jim Loats, Ph.D. – Calculus is a sink or swim subject. The authors approach calculus with humor to help you understand it all.

H

Math and Music: Harmonious Connections by Trudi Hammel Garland and Charity Vaughan Kahn – My friends who studied music in college tell me a lot of math knowledge is helpful to obtain a music degree. Here's an opportunity to combine music instruction with math.

H

Mathographics by Robert Dixon – Could be used for a high school math course, combining geometry, algebra, and trigonometry. Includes over 100 full-page drawings, exercises, and answers.

H

Agnesi To Zeno: Over 100 Vignettes from the History of Math by Sanderson Smith – Short vignettes of mathematicians and important discoveries, with activities for each. Would be a nice supplement to textbook learning – especially for girls as it contains several short biographies of important women in mathematics. However, you need to be on guard for political correctness.

M, H

The Joy of Mathematics: Discovering Mathematics All Around You by Theoni Pappas – Covering 147 topics, this book is designed to inspire future explorations. Not an in-depth study.

M, H

Mathematical Quilts: No Sewing Required! By Diana Venters and Elaine Krajenke Ellison – I bought this title for my daughter who loves to quilt. However, knowledge of quilting is not required to use this neat book about geometry. Lots of activities and teacher's notes.

M, H

Calculus by and for Young People by Don Cohen – Yes, this introduction to pre-calculus is a title for grade school. Take your time with it and use this opportunity to teach yourself calculus if need be. Best used with a group along with the teacher or parent. If you're on a tight budget, and can't find it at the library, skip the book (which is very tiny) and just get the worksheets.

G

Economics

Basic Economics: A Citizen's Guide to the Economy by Thomas Sowell – A Stanford professor of economics, Sowell writes a clear and concise explanation of economics for the layman. Follow up with *Economics in One Lesson.* My husband, who has a degree in economics, gave this book to our teenaged son when he expressed an interest in learning more about economics.

H, A

Economics in One Lesson: The Shortest and Surest Way to Understand Basic Economics by Henry Hazlitt – Short, readable chapters. The "one lesson" is taught in chapter one. The remaining chapters contain stories to back up the lesson.

H, A

The Math Behind Wall Street: How the Market Works and How to Make It Work for You by Nicholas

Teebagy – Outlines the concepts behind the stock market and explains the terminology. Gets down to basics.
H, A

The Road to Serfdom by F. A. Hayek – There are many books about Hayek's economics, but this is his most accessible book for a high school student. It's a critique of Europe's (particularly England's) shift to socialism after WWII. It contains much of his economic thinking, which is broader than purely economics and could easily be tied into history. If this sparks an interest, check out Hayek's other titles.
H, A

The Worldly Philosophers: The Lives, Times, and Ideas of the Great Economic Thinkers by Robert Heilbroner – Biographies of economists. Good for introducing economic concepts.
H, A

The Motley Fool Guide to Investing for Teens: Eight Steps to Having More Money than Your Parents Ever Dreamed of by David and Tom Gardner with Selena Maranjian – Teens learn investment strategies to prepare for their financial future. With wit, the authors share their advice on mutual funds, the stock market, IRA's, banking practices, and more.
H

Whatever Happened to Penny Candy? A Fast, Clear, and Fun Explanation of the Economics You Need For Success in Your Career, Business, and Investments **(Uncle Eric Book)** by Richard Maybury – Written from a Libertarian viewpoint, teaches basic economics using the correspondence from an uncle to his nephew. This book sparked a deep interest in economics in my sixteen-year-old son.
M, H

The Confe$$ions and $ecret$ of Howard J. Fingerhut by Esther Hershenhorn, illustrated by Ethan Long – A fun book written from the perspective of a fourth grade boy who starts a lawn care business for a school project.
G, M

The Story of Money by Betsy Maestro, illustrated by Gulio Mastro – From cave men, to ancient civilizations, to modern times. Learn about bartering, coins, paper money, and paperless money.
G

The Go-Around Dollar by Barbara Johnston Adams, illustrated by Joyce Audy Zarins – Follows a dollar bill as it travels from person to person.
P, G

Literature

Uncle Petros and Goldbach's Conjecture: A Novel of Mathematical Obsession by Apostolos Doxiadis – A fictional story of a mathematician who becomes obsessed with solving Goldbach's conjecture. An interesting read for both the mathematician and the math-phobe.
A, *

Fantasia Mathematica by Clifton Fadiman – Anthology of futuristic short stories. Brings imagination and fantasy to math. Note: there is one story of a man who fathers thirty children in one day to colonize Mars.
H, A, *

Flatland: A Romance of Many Dimensions by Edwin Abbott – In addition to being a novel that introduces the concepts of second, third, and fourth dimensions, it's a satire on society and class distinctions of Victorian England (first published in the 1880's).
H, A

The Parrot's Theorem: A Novel by Denis Guedj – Part
  murder mystery, part math history, this is an amusing
  introduction to mathematical discoveries.
  H, A, *

*Conned Again, Watson! Cautionary Tales of Logic, Math,
  and Probability* by Colin Bruce. Sherlock Holmes
  guides Watson and his clients through elementary
  mathematical reasoning.
  M, H

*The Man Who Counted: A Collection of Mathematical
  Adventures* by Malba Tahan – Takes place in thirteenth century Baghdad. A well-written novel introducing the reader to complex math puzzles in an interesting and fun way. Presents an opportunity to discuss
  Islam.
  M, H

A Gebra Named Al: A Novel by Wendy Isdell – Written by
  a 17-year-old girl who takes you on a journey through
  the Land of Mathematics.
  M

The Number Devil: A Mathematical Adventure by Hans
  Magnus Enzensberger, illustrated by Rotraut Susanne
  Berner, translated by Michael Henry Heim – Though it
  doesn't resemble a textbook in any way, shape, or
  form, this book does teach important math skills. I
  would read aloud to point out the author's mixed up
  theology when it comes to devils, heaven, and hell.
  M

Alice's Adventure in Wonderland by Lewis Carroll – See
  below.

Through the Looking Glass by Lewis Carroll – Carroll's
  books about Alice are not necessarily math literature,
  but they do contain a lot of logical problems to keep

their readers on their toes, with a little nonsense thrown in.

G, M, H

The Phantom Tollbooth by Norman Juster – A classic. More logic than arithmetic. Every child with math phobia should read this fun book about a boy who goes on an adventure that is filled with number and word puzzles.

G, M, H

Alvin's Secret Code by Clifford Hicks [Bethlehem Books] – Learn about cryptology and codes through a fun story. This reprint from forty years ago was loved by fourth graders everywhere. You may discover your children putting down the book to make their own invisible ink or creating secret codes.

G, M

The Dot and the Line: A Romance in Lower Mathematics by Norman Juster – A humorous tale about a straight line in love with a red dot, and the line's attempts to woo her away from a slothful squiggle.

G

Math Talk: Mathematical Ideas in Poems for Two Voices by Theoni Pappas – This is a creative way to teach math. The poems are designed to be read by two people simultaneously. Fun.

G

Picture Books

Fractals, Googols and Other Mathematical Tales by Theoni Pappas – A treasure trove of stories that make mathematical ideas come to life with an unusual cast of characters. Explores mathematical concepts and topics such as real numbers, exponents, dimensions, and geometry in both serious and humorous ways.

M, H

The Brown Paper School Series by Marilyn Burns, illustrated by Martha Weston – These are really fun books filled with puzzles and ideas that make math enjoyable for kids.
   The Book of Think
   The I Hate Mathematics! Book
   Math for Smarty Pants
     and more
   M

Fascinating Fibonacci: Mystery and Magic in Numbers by Trudi Hammel Garland – Share the wonder and awe of Fibonacci number sequences with your students.
   M

String, Straight-Edge, & Shadow: The Story of Geometry by Julia E. Diggins, illustrated by Corydon Bell – With nothing more than these three tools, men discovered the basic principles of elementary geometry. We enjoyed this as a read aloud.
   M

The Adventures of Penrose the Mathematical Cat by Theoni Pappas – Penrose, a cat with a knack for math, takes children on an adventurous tour of mathematical concepts from fractals to infinity.
   G, M

Anno's Mysterious Multiplying Jar by Masaichiro and Mitsumasa Anno – A very neat book that visually explains factorials.
   G, M

G Is for Googol: A Math Alphabet Book by David Schwartz, illustrated by Marissa Moss – Not all ABC books are for preschoolers, this book is definitely for the older child. Presents complicated math concepts in a fun and colorful way.
   G, M

Melisande by E. Nesbit, illustrated by P. J. Lynch –
Fairytale about a princess cursed to be bald. Later, she
is granted one wish. Mayhem takes over when she
wishes for golden hair a yard long that grows an inch
every day and twice as fast when it's cut. Do the math.
G, M

Murderous Maths Series by Kjartan Poskitt – This is a
colorful and funny series from England. You'll forget
math is supposed to be boring or difficult.
Do You Feel Lucky: The Secrets of Probability
The Fiendish Angletron
Murderous Math
Numbers: Keys to the Universe
The Phantom X
and more.
G, M

Amanda Bean's Amazing Dream: A Mathematical Story
by Cindy Neuschwander – Amanda's dream shows
children the why and how of multiplication.
G

The Grapes of Math: Mind Stretching Math Riddles by
Greg Tang, illustrated by Harry Briggs – Teaches children creative ways to use patterns and combinations of
numbers to solve math puzzles quickly and effectively.
G

The History of Counting by Denise Schmandt-Besserat,
illustrated by Michael Hayes – Beautifully illustrated,
this book traces the invention of number systems.
Easy to tie into your history studies.
G

One Grain of Rice by Demi – Tells the story of a selfish
Raja in India and the village girl who outsmarts him
using math skills. The Raja learns an important lesson
about selfishness as well as a lesson about the power

of doubling. As with all of Demi's books, the illustrations are beautiful.

G

Roman Numerals I to M: Numerabilia Romania Uno Ad Duo Mila: Liber De Difficillimo Computando Numerum by Arthur Geisert – I taught my children Roman numerals with this fun pictorial. Roman numerals are represented by illustrations of little pink pigs. For I there is one pig and for MM there are 2,000 pigs on the page. Visual learners will love this.

G

Tiger Math: Learning to Graph from a Baby Tiger by Ann Whitehead Nagda and Cindy Bickel – True story of a Siberian tiger cub, born into captivity, who quits eating. Learn about picture, circle, bar, and line graphs as you watch T.J. finally start eating, thanks to the attention of his keepers.

G

Wild Fibonacci: Nature's Secret Code Revealed by Joy Hulme – Don't be afraid to introduce seemingly complex ideas to young children (or yourself). This Fibonacci counting book has beautiful artwork.

G

Anno's Magic Seeds by Mitsumasa Anno – Neat book, which teaches thrift as well as math.

P, G

Domino Addition by Lynette Long, Ph.D. – Learn simple addition with dominoes.

P, G

Grandfather Tang's Story: A Tale Told with Tangrams by Ann Tompert – Tangrams are ancient Chinese puzzles, which are popular today with teachers who use math manipulatives.

P, G

How Much is a Million by David Schwartz – A fun book, which helps children understand the immensity of numbers. Also available as a Reading Rainbow video.
P, G

Marvelous Math: A Book of Poems edited by Lee Bennett Hopkins and Rebecca Davis, illustrated by Karen Barbour – A great way to look at math: through poetry.
P, G

Math Curse by John Scieszke, illustrated by Lane Smith – The central character is afflicted with a "math curse," which makes her see everything as a math problem.
P, G

Math-terpieces by Greg Tang – Now here is an interesting concept: combining art appreciation with your math studies.
P, G

On Beyond a Million: An Amazing Math Journey by David Schwartz, illustrated by Paul Meisel – Professor X. P. Nential demonstrates counting from one to a googol by using exponents. He throws in some interesting facts at the same time. (Did you know the Earth weighs about 13 septillion pounds?)
P, G

Pigs in a Blanket: Fun With Math and Time by Amy Axelrod, illustrated by Sharon McGinley-Nally – The abstract concept of time is made delightfully fun here as the Pig family races the clock to get to the beach.
P, G

Pigs in the Pantry: Fun with Math and Cooking – by Amy Axelrod, illustrated by Sharon McGinley-Nally – The pig family gets all mixed up when they try to make chili. Includes the recipe so you and the children can do it right.
P, G

Math

Pigs Will Be Pigs: Fun with Math and Money by Amy
Axelrod, illustrated by Sharon McGinley-Nally – This
time, the Pig Family teaches about money as they turn
their house upside down to find enough money to eat
out after finding the refrigerator bare.
P, G

A Remainder of One by Elinor Pinczes – An easy introduction to the concept of remainders.
P, G

***Twelve Snails to One Lizard: A Tale of Mischief and
Measurement*** by Susan Hightower, illustrated by Matt
Novak – A silly story about beavers, bullfrogs, and
more. Teaches children the concepts of measurement.
P, G

Puzzle/Coloring/Comic Books

Games for Math by Peggy Kaye – Written for parents and
teachers. Sixty-six game ideas for kindergarten
through third grade.
A

The Cartoon Guide to Statistics by Larry Gonick –
Though a comic book, this is a title for the teen or
advanced student.
H, A

***The Colossal Book of Mathematics: Classic Puzzles,
Paradoxes, and Problems*** by Martin Gardner – This
huge volume begins with simple puzzles and then
guides you through the complex. Covers a wide range
of topics from fractals to four dimensions to topology
and so much more.
H, A

The Snark Puzzle Book by Martin Gardner – Based on
Lewis Carroll's nonsense poem *The Hunting of the
Snark*. Who says you can't tie math into poetry? The

puzzles are challenging.

M, H, A

Lewis Carroll's Games and Puzzles by Lewis Carroll, Edward Wakeling – In addition to being a children's writer, Lewis Carroll was a mathematician.

G, M, H, A

Math Trek: Adventures in the MathZone by Ivars Peterson and Nancy Henderson – MathZone is an amusement park filled with fun math activities, tricks, and puzzles.

G, M

Anno's Math Games by Mitsumasa Anno – If you like this fun book, make sure to check out the two sequels.

G

The Multiplication Tables Colouring Book: Solve the Puzzle Pictures While Learning Your Tables by Hilary McElderry – Great for reinforcing multiplication skills. I use this for all my children.

G

Historical Timeline

Pythagoras (c.582-507 BC), Greece

What's Your Angle Pythagoras? A Math Adventure by Julie Ellis – Great fictional story of Pythagoras' childhood. Presents the Pythagorean Theorem through an appealing story. Easy for grade school children to understand.

G

Euclid (c. 300 BC), Greece

Euclid's Elements – Euclid's famous 13 books. Start with the definitions before going to the introduction. For advanced students.

H, A

Eratosthenes (287-192 BC), Greece

The Librarian Who Measured the Earth by Kathryn
    Lasky – A beautiful picture book about the Greek who
    was able to estimate the circumference of the earth
    without modern technology. Fascinating.
    P, G

The Rosetta Stone (196 BC), Egypt

The Riddle of the Rosetta Stone by James Cross Giblin –
    It took scholars more than a hundred years to translate
    the Rosetta Stone. Though not a mathematics book per
    se, *Riddle* introduces the reader to the importance of
    logic.
    G, M

King Arthur (c. 537), England

Sir Cumference Series by Cindy Neuschwander, illustrat-
    ed by Wayne Geehan – A fun series and a fun play on
    words.
    Sir Cumference and the First Round Table
    Sir Cumference and the Dragon of Pi
    Sir Cumference and the Sword in the Cone
    Sir Cumference and the Great Knight of Angleland
    P, G

Pierre de Fermat (1601-1665) France

*Fermat's Enigma: The Epic Quest to Solve the World's
    Greatest Puzzle* by Simon Singh – Fermat wrote his
    famous formula in the margins of his notes, but did
    not provide the proof. It took 350 years (1993) to
    finally prove it.
    H, A

Blaise Pascal (1623-1662), France

Pensees, Christianity for Modern Pagans edited by Peter
    Kreeft [Ignatius] – Catholic author Peter Kreeft adds
    his commentary to Pascal's apology.
    H, A, ✠

Ben Franklin (1706-1790), U.S.

Ben Franklin and the Magic Squares **(A Step into Reading + Math)** – Discusses Franklin's discoveries and how the "magic squares" came about. Gives you a "Make Your Own Magic Square" at the back of the book.

P, G

Benjamin Banneker (1731-1806), U.S.

Molly Bannaky by Alice McGill – The story of Banneker's grandmother.

G

What Are You Figuring Now? A Story about Benjamin Banneker by Jeri Ferris – A self-taught African American astronomer and mathematician, Banneker is an inspiration.

G

Alan Turing, (1912-1954), England

Turing and the Computer **(The Big Idea Series)** by Paul Strathern - An overview of Alan Turing whose brilliant mathematical imagination laid the foundation for computers as we know them today. This book should be read by parents first as it deals with Turing's homosexuality.

H, A, *

History

Though I didn't enjoy history as a subject when I was a student, I have grown to love it as an adult. This love grew when I found myself reading historical literature in order to educate myself so I could, in turn, educate my children. This led me to put aside the textbooks of my youth and replace them with *real* books in teaching my own children. As a result, history is not only my children's favorite subject, but also the favorite subject of the home-schooled children who join us once a week for a history co-op in my home.

I have structured our co-op so the children read historical fiction and biographies, concentrating heavily on the lives of the saints, and present a book report. To keep things interesting, we sometimes forgo traditional book reports and do fun projects such as lap books, dioramas, short plays, etc. The point is to have the children share what they learned with the other children. I do this for two reasons. One, we all retain lessons better when we teach. In sharing their books with the other students, they are in essence, teaching. The other reason for the book reports, or book report alternatives, is each child has something unique to share since they're all reading different books. Sometimes, the other children will discover a book they would like to read simply for enjoyment.

I do use Catholic history textbooks, but only as supplemental material, reading aloud from them and following with a round-table discussion. Using a textbook as a spine helps children pull together the lessons learned from their individual books into one big picture.

I use *For the Love of Literature* alongside *Catholic World History Timeline and Guide* by Marcia Neill (available from www.rchistory.com). It ties everything together nicely for us. The children love pasting pictures of the peo-

History

📄 **Top Ten Book Report Alternatives**

Based on the book you just read, do one of the following:
10. Write a one-act play.
9. Write an echo story.
8. Write an ad - talk others into reading your book.
7. Make a map - show where the story's events took place.
6. Create artwork, depicting scenes from the book.
5. Create a timeline - show when the events of the book took place.
4. Write a poem expressing your feelings about the book.
3. Write a magazine review.
2. Create a movie poster based on the book. Don't forget to cast the main characters.
1. Present a newscast.

These are just a few ideas. Use your imagination and add to this list.

ple and events from their studies to the timeline. If you do decide to use the *Catholic World History Timeline and Guide*, I suggest taking the timeline and pictures to an office or teacher's store to be laminated. It's designed to be used from grade school to high school, so you'll want it to stay in good condition. It's an expensive program, but when I factor in the number of children times the number of years we homeschool, it becomes a thrifty choice.

If you prefer to make your own timeline, it's easy to do. See www.maureenwittmann.com to download a free template. For pictures to place on the timeline, have the children draw their own, search the Internet, or cut out pictures from old encyclopedias purchased at thrift stores or garage sales.

Having a timeline helps my children understand the order and flow of history. Just as a book has a beginning, a middle, and an end, so does history. It's important children understand when historical events take place in perspective to other important events. A timeline provides a visual presentation of how history is ordered. It also gives children a multi-sensory approach to history to help them retain their lessons, touching and seeing history.

As our studies progress, we tape pictures to the timeline. I know one family who scans the covers of the books they read and then tapes those pictures to their timeline. You could also find pictures of the book covers at publishers' websites. I think this is a terrific idea and really completes the concept of teaching history through literature.

If you don't have the wall space for an extensive timeline, you have another option. The children can create a Book of Centuries, which is a timeline in a notebook or three-ring binder. Again, you can use the *Catholic World History Timeline and Guide*, or make your own with templates found at www.maureenwittmann.com.

I continue to read adult history books so I am able to speak knowledgeably, and also because it encourages the children when they see that I, too, have a desire to accumulate knowledge. Keep one step ahead of your children by reading the assigned books or texts yourself. At the very least, skim-read them. If the children are studying the Revolutionary War, your personal reading should be the War of 1812. By the time the children get to 1812, you'll be reading about the Civil War. Doing this will keep the information fresh on your mind so you can guide your children through their studies.

We also pray novenas to the saints we're studying at the time. Individual novenas can be found by searching the Internet, checking with your favorite Catholic bookstore, or reading books on novenas such as *Mention Your Request Here* [Our Sunday Visitor] by Michael Dubruiel.

History

History is central to our academic studies, and brings all of our subjects together. Since history is an accounting of everything mankind has accomplished throughout time, it's easy to tie in other subjects. Art, music, geography, language arts, science, and even math can be integrated with the study of history. This can be done by researching popular art, listening to music, and reading biographies of famous scientists and mathematicians of the era. Language arts are addressed by reading period literature and writing book reports. I take new words from our history class and add them to our vocabulary and spelling lessons. To meet the special interests of my children, we've looked into the architecture, clothing, medical practices, and eating habits of differing regions and periods of history. We've even acted out a dramatic play from Catholic Heritage Curricula.

Religion is the easiest of subjects to tie into history, for without God there is no history. His impact cannot be denied. We always discuss religious beliefs of the era and how those beliefs are different or similar to our own. We also discuss the impact individuals have had on history and how their religious beliefs worked for the betterment or detriment of society. Perhaps most importantly, we talk about how we personally, as children of God, have an impact on history.

Finally, in *A Vote of Thanks to Cyrus*, Dorothy Sayers relates that as a child she discovered the Cyrus mentioned in her Bible was the very same Cyrus found in her history textbook. Bible stories are not mere tales to entertain, but in fact history. Talk about Jesus Christ as a historical figure and the impact Christianity has had in shaping world events.

📄 Top Ten Supplemental Ideas for History

10. For preschool- and grade school-aged children look for Mary Fabyan Windeatt coloring books [TAN], Pauline Comics series, or Fr. Lovasik storybooks (Catholic Book Publishing) on the Saints.

9. Check out Usborne books and kits, as well as Bellerphon and Dover coloring books, paper dolls, and cutouts.

8. Play Telephone, Hangman, or Finish the Sentence to reinforce lessons learned.

7. Develop word search and crossword puzzles (free service at www.puzzlemaker.com).

6. Listen to music of the era as you study.

5. See Life of Christ Timeline by Sister Elizabeth Ann, Catholics in American History, and other free downloads at www.catholichomeschooling.com.

4. Check the Internet or library for ancient maps, and always have a globe on hand.

3. Many of the literary suggestions are also available as audio books. These are especially great for long car rides and for auditory learners.

2. Look up CCC (Catechism of the Catholic Church) references. These are listed in *Catholic World History Timeline and Guide*.

1. Search out primary documents (original sources), especially in the high school years. The Internet History Sourcebook Project at www.fordham.edu/halsall/ provides a good beginning. Vatican documents can be found at www.cwtn.com or www.rc.net/rcchurch/vat-stmts.

Textbooks:

Christ the King, Lord of History by Dr. Anne Carroll [TAN] – Catholic high school Ancient history text. H, ✠

Christ and the Americas by Dr. Anne Carroll [TAN] – Catholic high school American history text. H, ✠

Catholic Textbook Project [www.catholictextbookproject.com] – This appealing history and social studies series takes a story-telling approach. Once complete, there will be twelve textbooks. Though written for Catholic schools, could be used in a homeschool setting.

From Sea to Shining Sea: The Story of America – Grades 5 to 9.

All Ye Lands: World Cultures and Geography – Grades 6 to 9.

A Light to the Nations: Christian Civilization – Grades 7 to 11.

One Nation Under God: The American Achievement – Grades 7 to 12.

M, H, ✠

The Evangelization of the New World: Hispanic Influence in American History by Dr. James R. Leek [St. Paul's Publishing] – Catholic middle/high school American history text, focusing on the Spanish influence.

M, H, ✠

Land of Our Lady Series [Neumann] – Catholic middle school texts. Reprinted from the 1950's.

Founders of Freedom –Ancient history. Grade 4.

Bearers of Freedom – Discovery, exploration, and settlement of America. Grade 5.

Leaders of Freedom – Colonial America through the early 1800's. Grade 6.

Challenge of Freedom – Through the Civil War and Reconstruction. Grade 7.

Guardian of Freedom – Through the 1950's. Grade 8. M, ✠

The Old World and America by Bishop Furlong [TAN] – Catholic middle school Ancient history text. M, ✠

Our Pioneers and Patriots by Bishop Furlong [TAN] – Catholic middle school American history text. M, ✠

Overview

How the Catholic Church Built Western Civilization by Thomas E. Woods, Jr. Ph.D. [Regnery] – Should the Middle Ages be referred to as the Dark Ages? Or was it a time when civilization flourished? This book focuses on the Catholic Church and the positive force it's been to civilization. H, A, ✠

The Politically Incorrect Guide to American History by Thomas E. Woods, Jr., Ph.D. – Woods, *Latin Mass Magazine* associate editor, sets out to correct the liberal bias that often permeates American history textbooks. H, A

The World's Great Speeches: 292 Speeches from Pericles to Nelson Mandela – Includes speeches from ancient eras to modern day. Reading the speeches of world leaders is a great way to learn about a culture. H, A

Our Sunday Visitor's Encyclopedia of Catholic History by Matthew Bunson [Our Sunday Visitor] – A great reference book to keep on your shelf. M, H, A, ✠

History

Reading Comprehension: Stories of the Saints, Volumes I, II, III, and IV by Elaine Woodfield [Catholic Heritage Curricula] – Short biographies of saints, along with reading comprehension questions, vocabulary words, and activities to reinforce lessons. Also includes writing exercises.
M, ✠

Great Moments in Catholic History [Neumann] – Chronological stories of historical events.
G, M, ✠

Heroes of God's Church [Neumann] – Lives of the saints.
G, M, ✠

Heroes of Virtue: A Timeline-Manual of New World Saints and Blesseds [Catholic Heritage Curricula] – Lives of the saints in the Americas, plus activities.
G, M, ✠

Butler's Lives of the Saints – The lives of the saints are a great way to study history. Choose saints who lived during the time period you are studying and read their biography.
G, M, H, A, ✠

Praise Him with Your Very Life: A Collection of Plays [Catholic Heritage Curricula] – This is a fun way to learn history, through drama. We acted out a few of these plays on the lives of the saints in our history co-op.
G, M, ✠

What People Wore: 1,800 Illustrations from Ancient Times to the Early Twentieth Century by Douglas Gorsline – We enjoyed this book. There is a lot to learn about a culture by their dress.
G, M, H

Other

Unit Studies:

ABC's of Christian Culture by Julia Fogassy [Our
Father's House] – Available in two levels, each covering the same ten time periods (from ancient to modern) with Level B covering the material more in depth.
Timeline and mapping activities, hands-on projects,
and research assignments. Ages 10 to 17.
G, M, H, ✠

Connecting with History: A Catholic Guide to History
by Sonya Romens [RCHistory] – Two volumes currently available (*A Guide to Salvation History* and *The
Founding of the Kingdom*), with more volumes in pro-
duction. Coordinates multiple grade levels, K-12.
Students study the same topic, but at their own skill
level. Based on a four-year cycle, using the Bible,
Catholic texts, and literature.
G, M, H, ✠

History Links [Wooly Lamb] – Units currently available
include General Studies, Ancient Mesopotamia,
Ancient Egypt, Ancient Israel, Ancient Greece,
Ancient Rome, and Medieval, with other units in pro-
duction. Research projects and hands-on activities for
preschool to high school, using Scripture, papal
encyclicals, the Catechism of the Catholic Church, and
an encyclopedia.
P, G, M, H, ✠

Syllabi:

**Syllabus for American History using 'Christ and the
Americas'** by Laura Berquist [Emmanuel Books] –
Provides daily lesson plans for thirty-two weeks.
H, ✠

Syllabus for Ancient History using 'The Founding of Christendom' by Laura Berquist [Emmanuel Books] – Provides daily lesson plans for thirty-two weeks. H, ✠

Audio Stories:

Jim Weiss – I have a child who is not a reader, but a listener. Story teller Jim Weiss is great for listening. Through GreathallProductions.com.

CatholicWorldMission.org – The audios of their Glory Stories (lives of the saints) can be heard on EWTN or can be purchased at their website.

NorthernRain.tv – Produces audio versions of Bethlehem titles such as *Enemy Brothers* and *The Story of Rolf and the Viking Bow* as well as an audio play called *Perpetua's Choice,* which is quite nice.

Historical Timeline
Old Testament/Ancient Israel

The Bible – *The Catholic World History Timeline and Guide* (see appendix) provides Scripture references to accompany historical events of the Bible. Use a good Scripture study alongside your Bible reading. We use *The Great Bible Adventure: A Journey Through the Bible,* a video series by Jeff Cavins [Ascension] with two other families.
G, M, H, A, ✠

Navarre Bible Commentary: Pentateuch [Sceptor] – The first five books of the Old Testament using the Revised Standard Version, Catholic Edition. Contains both the English and Latin text plus commentaries. The commentaries draw on Church documents, the exegesis of Fathers and Doctors of the Church, and works of contemporary spiritual writers, particularly

St. Josemaría Escrivá, who initiated the Navarre Bible project and founded Opus Dei.

H, A, ✠

Introduction to the Bible by Fr. John Laux [TAN] – Originally published in 1932, Fr. Laux uses the Douay-Rheims Bible for his introduction.

H, A, ✠

Antiquities of the Jews by Josephus – Interpretations and traditions of the Old Testament by Josephus, a late first century Pharisee and historian.

H, A

Teen Guide to the Bible by Alfred McBride, O. Praem. [Our Sunday Visitor] – Salvation history and the life of Christ for teenagers. Discussion questions included, making it easy to use with your student.

H, ✠

Bible History by Fr. Ignatius Schuster [TAN] – Used in Catholic schools for years, covers the most famous events in the Old and New Testaments.

M, ✠

The Bible for Young Catholics [Pauline] – The Bible retold for grade school children.

G, ✠

Child's Bible History by F. J. Knecht [TAN] – An abridged version of Schuster's *Bible History* for grade school children.

G, ✠

Creation

Perelandra by C. S. Lewis – The second book in Lewis' Space Trilogy. Discuss the similarities between Lewis' science fiction and the reality of Genesis.

H

The Magician's Nephew by C. S. Lewis – The first book in The Chronicles of Narnia. Discuss the similarities

between Aslan's creation of Narnia and God's creation of Earth.
G, M

Noah (c.2944-1994 BC)

Noah and the Ark by Tomie dePaola – A simple picture book, tells the story of Noah, his ark, and the Great Flood.
P, G

Abraham (c. 1991-1816 BC)
Isaac (c.1891-1711 BC)

The Binding of Isaac by Barbara Cohen, illustrated by Charles Mikolaycak – The story of when God commands Abraham to sacrifice his son Isaac. What makes this book special is that the story is told by Isaac when he is a grandfather.
G

Joseph (c.1750-1640 BC)

Joseph the Dreamer by Clyde Robert Bulla, illustrated by Gordon Laite – Rich in detail, this is a complete telling of Joseph's story. Joseph is Isaac's grandson – look for the grandchildren mentioned in *The Binding of Isaac.*
G

Hittite Empire (1600-1200 BC)

Hittite Warrior **(Living History Library)** by Joanne Williamson [Bethlehem] – Circa 1200 BC Judea, Uriah the Hittite leaves his conquered homeland and eventually finds himself in a great battle between the Canaanite forces of Sisera and the Hebrew forces of Barak.
M, H, ✠

David (c. 971 BC)

King David and His Songs: A Story of the Psalms by
Mary Fabyan Windeatt [TAN] – We enjoy Windeatt's
books as read alouds. This title chronicles King David
and his rise from shepherd boy to King of Israel.
G, M, ✠

Jonah (c. 786-746 BC)

Jonah and the Great Fish by Clyde Robert Bulla, illustrated by Helga Aichinger – Adds a few extra details,
but a very nice retelling.
P, G

King Hezekiah (c.715-686 BC)

God King: A Story in the Days of King Hezekiah (Living
History Library) by Joanne Williamson [Bethlehem]
– Taking place in 701 BC, this story's foundation is
from the Biblical account of King Hezekiah in the
book of Isaiah.
G, M, ✠

Nehemiah (?-433 BC)

Victory on the Walls: A Story of Nehemiah by Frieda
Clark Hyman [Bethlehem] – Takes place in 445 BC
when Judaism was re-established in the Promise Land.
Daring adventures abound when a 13-year-old boy
leaves Persia with his Uncle Nehemiah to return to
Jerusalem.
G, M, ✠

Ancient Egypt

The Pharaohs of Ancient Egypt (Landmark Books) by
Elizabeth Payne – Discusses the life and history of
ancient Egypt, from earliest times through the reign of

Ramses II, as it has been pieced together from the
work of archaeologists.
M, H

***Pharaohs & Pyramids* (Time Traveler Series)** by Tony
Allan – Through its simple text and drawings, this
Usborne book explains the daily life of the ancient
Egyptians, including their agriculture and religion.
G, M

***Ancient Egypt* (DK Eyewitness)** – This series combines
lots of interesting color photographs and drawings
with bite-size snippets of history. I use these books for
easy narrations.
G, M

***Desert* (DK Eyewitness)** – Photo essay of deserts, mainly
in northern Africa and the Middle East. I used this title
when we studied the ancient Egyptians because the
desert played such an important role in their daily life.
G, M

***Pyramid* (DK Eyewitness)** – Covers pyramids all over the
world, but a large focus is on the Egyptian tombs.
Full-color photographs as opposed to drawings.
G, M

***Pyramid* by David Macaulay** – Macaulay shows, through
great detail, how the great pharaohs' burial places
were conceived and constructed. As with his other
books, his draftsmanship is superb. Also introduces
the ancient Egyptians' philosophy of life and death.
G, M

***The Egyptian Cinderella* by Shirley Climo** – I once put
together a Cinderella unit study where the children and
I read Cinderella stories from many different countries
and cultures. Incredibly, it gave the children a strong
awareness of the differences between cultures.
P, G

History

Pharaoh Sekenenre III (c. 1590 BC)

Shadow Hawk (**Living History Library**) by Andre Norton [Bethlehem] – This is a dramatic story filled with secret plots, dangerous undercover missions, and daring military campaigns.

H, ✠

Queen Hatshepsut (?-1468 BC)

Mara, Daughter of the Nile by Eloise Jarvis McGraw – The story of an ingenious Egyptian slave girl who undertakes a dangerous assignment as a spy in the royal palace of Thebes during the rule of Queen Hatshepsut.

M

Pharaoh Amenhotep III (1417-1379 BC)

The Golden Goblet by Eloise Jarvis McGraw – Exciting story of Ranofer, a young Egyptian orphan, who overcomes abuse and reveals a hideous crime, reshaping his own destiny.

M

Pharaoh Tutankhamen (1343-1325 BC)

Tut's Mummy Lost – And Found (**Step-Into-Reading, Step 4**) by Judy Donnelly – A simple picture book detailing how King Tut was buried as well as the ancient Egyptians' beliefs about death.

G

Moses (c. 1250 BC)

The Cat of Bubastes: A Tale of Ancient Egypt by G. A. Henty – The main character accidentally kills a cat, an act of sacrilege to the ancient Egyptians punishable by death. He flees and finds himself embarking on quite the adventure. Moses makes a cameo appearance.

Note: Some of Henty's other titles contain anti-Catholic bias.

M, H

Queen Cleopatra (69-30 BC)

Antony and Cleopatra by William Shakespeare – Don't miss the opportunity to introduce your teenagers to the Bard while studying history.

H, A

Cleopatra by Diane Stanley and Peter Vennema – Queen of Egypt at the age of eighteen, Cleopatra's passion was to conquer the world. A timeless story of love, war, and ambition. This pictorial biography is entertaining and educational. Note: Stanley's biography of Queen Elizabeth, *Good Queen Bess*, contains anti-Catholic bias.

G, M

Ancient Greece

The Greek Way by Edith Hamilton – A collection of essays explaining why the Greeks are important to today's world.

H, A

D'Aulaire's Book of Greek Myths by Ingri and Edgar d'Aulaire – I recommend this classic on audio to hear the correct pronunciations of the Greek names.

G, M

Ancient Greece **(DK Eyewitness)** – Photo essay of the ancient Greeks. Learn the history of their culture, philosophy, science, medicine, and the role geography played.

G, M

I Wonder Why Greeks Built Temples by Fiona MacDonald – An introduction to ancient Greece through a question-and-answer format. My children enjoy the I Wonder Why Series.

G, M

How We Learned the Earth is Round by Patricia Lauber – Explains how perceptions of the earth's shape have changed since early times. Also describes the reasoning that led the ancient Greeks to conclude the earth is round. A simple explanation of a rather complex idea.

G

Homer (c. 800BC)

The Iliad by Homer – This 2,700-year-old epic poem still stirs the heart. Heroism abounds with men wrestling with deep emotions and battling through the devastation and destruction of war. A classic, but can be a task to get through for the less-than-scholarly student.

H, A

Odyssey by Homer – Simply stated, this is the story of everyman's journey though life. Odysseus must rely on his wit for survival as he encounters extraordinary forces during his ten-year voyage home to Ithaca after the Trojan War.

H, A

The Children's Homer: The Adventures of Odysseus and the Tale of Troy by Padriac Colum – A 1965 retelling of Homer's *The Iliad* and *The Odyssey* for children. The language and vocabulary can be challenging, but worth the effort.

M

Black Ships Before Troy: The Story of the Iliad by Rosemary Sutcliff – A modern retelling of *The Illiad*. It's the story of the Trojan War, from the quarrel for the golden apple, and the flight of Helen with Paris, to the destruction of Troy.

M

The Wanderings of Odysseus: The Story of the Odyssey
by Rosemary Sutcliff – The story of Odysseus' long
years of wandering after the Trojan War. Sutcliff's
retelling makes a nice read aloud. One may say
Odysseus' story is that of everyone's search for home.
M

The Trojan Horse: How the Greeks Won the War (Step-
Into-Reading, Step 5)** by Emily Little – This picture
book is an account of the way the Greeks tricked the
Trojans and rescued Helen of Troy.
G

Aesop (c. 600 BC)
Aesop's Fables – When we studied the Ancient Greeks we
began each lesson with a fable from *Aesop*. Not history per se, but great moral lessons transcending history.
P, G, M

Aeschylus of Athens (525-456 BC)
The Oresteian Trilogy by Aeschylus – This is a classic set
of tragedies centering on the royal family of Argos,
and set off by Clytemnestra, the backstabbing wife of
Agamemnon. For the advanced student.
H, A

Sophocles of Athens (496-406 BC)
The Theban Plays by Sophocles – These 2,500-year-old
plays have easily withstood the test of time. Reading
the original works of the Greeks is recommended to
students seeking a classical education.
H, A

Persian Wars (490-479 BC)
Herodotus of Halicarnassus (c. 484-425 BC)
History of the Persian Wars by Herodotus – Herodotus is
known as the "Father of History" even though some
inaccuracies can be found in his work. He presents an
in-depth look into the Persian Wars. Though thousands
of years old, this work is readable for an advanced
middle-school student.
M, H, A

Golden Age of Athens (479-430 BC)
*The Golden Fleece: And the Heroes Who Lived Before
Achilles* by Padriac Colum – Colum weaves the tales
of Jason and the Argonauts with classic Greek mythol-
ogy, creating a captivating epic.
M, H

Socrates (470-399 BC)
*Philosophy 101 by Socrates: An Introduction to
Philosophy Via Plato's Apology* by Peter Kreeft
[Ignatius] – This book spurred an interest in several
teens I know. Great book.
H, A, X

Peloponnesian War (431-405 BC)
The History of the Peloponnesian War by Thucydides –
Along with Herodotus, Thucydides is considered one
of the first great historians. His history of the war
between Athens and Sparta is one of the most brilliant
histories of all times and contains a keen political
insight.
H, A

Plato (428-347 BC)

Apology by Plato – Foundational reading for the student of Western philosophy. All the big themes of the Greeks are covered: the gods, truth, wisdom, and death.
H, A

The Dialogues of Plato – Socrates did not leave behind any written works, but his preeminent student Plato did. Here, Plato creates dialogues with Socrates on the questions we all desire answered: what is love, virtue, and so on.
H, A

The Republic by Plato – Plato's classic work of political thought and how a society should function.
H, A

The Right Way to Live: Plato's Republic for Catholic Students by Richard Geraghty, foreword by Rhonda Chervin [CMJ Marian] – This is a must read for any student of Plato.
H, A, ✠

Aristotle (384-322 BC)

The Poetics by Aristotle – Aristotle observes and sets out the qualities necessary for the writing of epics and tragedies. In the end, he established concepts that have since become the cornerstones of Western dramatic and literary practice.
H, A

Ancient Rome

The Founding of Christendom **(History of Christendom, vol.1)** by Warren H. Carroll [Christendom] – First in a series, that in its whole is a comprehensive narrative of Western history written from an orthodox Catholic perspective. This volume covers 9,000 BC to 324 AD.
H, A, ✠

Detectives in Togas by Henry Winterfield – This is a fun book to introduce young students to Ancient Rome, especially if they enjoy mysteries.
G, M

Ancient Rome (**DK Eyewitness**) – Photo essay of the ancient Romans and their empire.
G, M

City: A Story of Roman Planning and Construction by David Macaulay – Shows the planning and building of an imaginary Roman city. Macaulay focuses on the achievement of efficient and rational city planning. The drawings are superb. You may need to discuss the pagan ritual that takes place in the beginning.
G, M

Julius Caesar (100-44 BC)

Julius Caesar by William Shakespeare – Antony's speech is cited as the one of the finest speeches in history, despite being entirely fiction. Still, this is a must read. Shakespeare is of course brilliant in sharing this tale of honor and betrayal.
H, A

Commentaries on the Gallic War by Julius Caesar – Look for a version with notes, maps, and other helpful information. Text can also be found free on the Internet.
H, A

Caesar's Gallic War by Olivia Coolidge – Historical fiction story of the Gallic War (58 to 51 BC), narrated by a fictitious soldier in Caesar's army. More readable to the younger student than Caesar's *Commentaries on the Gallic War*.
M, H

Julius Caesar by Robert Green – Fact-filled biography with detailed pictures and maps.
G, M

History

Augustus Caesar (27 BC-14 AD)

Augustus Caesar's World by Genevieve Foster – This is an enjoyable read presenting not only the story of Augustus Caesar, but the stories of all the other events going on during the lifetime of Caesar, including the birth of Christ (though from a secular viewpoint). I found the pictures to be perfect to use on our timeline. Note: several of Foster's other titles are problematic in their depiction of Christianity.

M, H

The Blessed Mother

Mary: God's Yes to Man, Encyclical Letter of John Paul II: Mother of the Redeemer by Joseph Cardinal Ratzinger [Ignatius] – A compelling and deep study of the Blessed Mother's role in history and in the Church.

H, A, ✠

Roses, Fountains and Gold: The Virgin Mary in History, Art, Music, Apparition by John Martin [Ignatius] – Encompasses Mary's influence not only on history and theology, but in art and music. Also, apparitions are explored to demonstrate Mary's work did not end when she gave birth to Jesus.

H, A, ✠

Mary, the Mother of Jesus by Tomie de Paola – People seem to either love or hate de Paola's artwork. I personally love his books. This particular title is beautifully illustrated and reverent to Our Lady.

G, ✠

The Life of Christ (c.0-33 AD)

The Bible – *The Catholic World History Timeline and Guide* (see appendix) provides Scripture references to accompany historical events of the Bible. Use a good

Scripture study alongside your Bible reading. We use *The Great Bible Adventure: A Journey through the Bible* video series by Jeff Cavins [Ascension] with two other families.

G, M, H, A, ✠

Navarre Bible Commentaries: ***New Testament*** [Sceptor] – The New Testament using the Revised Standard Version, Catholic Edition. Contains both the English and Latin text plus commentaries. The commentaries draw on Church documents, the exegesis of the Fathers and Doctors of the Church, and works of contemporary spiritual writers – particularly St. Josemaría Escrivá, who initiated the Navarre Bible project and founded Opus Dei.

H, A, ✠

The Spear: A Novel of the Crucifixion by Louis de Wohl [Ignatius] – One of my favorite novels. The de Wohl historical fiction books are reprints from the 1940's and '50's. This title tells the story of a hardened Roman centurion named Longinus. Tradition tells us Longinus is the one who pierced Christ's side at the crucifixion.

H, A, ✠

The Robe by Lloyd Douglass – A Roman soldier wins Christ's robe as a gambling prize. He then sets forth on a quest to find Truth. This wonderful story of adventure, faith, romance, and redemption, was made into a famous movie.

H, A

The Bronze Bow by Elizabeth George Speare – This story, set in Galilee during Jesus' lifetime, is about a young Jewish rebel who is won over to the gentle teachings of Christ.

M

A Life of Our Lord for Children by Marigold Hunt
[Sophia] – Hunt is a master storyteller. She engages
the reader and brings the Bible to life.
G, M, ✠

God's Love Story by Poor Clare Nuns [Catholic Heritage
Curricula] – This is a beautiful way to tell the story of
God's plan for creation and salvation, in the form of a
bedtime story. Based on the Bible.
G, ✠

The Miracles of Jesus by Tomie de Paola – Children can't
help but fall even more in love with Jesus after reading this beautifully illustrated book.
G, ✠

The Birth of the Church (c.33)

The Fathers of the Church (**Expanded Edition**) by Mike
Aquilina [Our Sunday Visitor] – The author brings
understanding to the Early Church Fathers, using their
own words.
H, A, ✠

The Grail Code: Quest for the Real Presence by Michael
Aquilina and Christopher Bailey [Loyola] – A wonder-
ful, historical look into the cup of Jesus.
H, A, ✠

The Mass of the Early Christians by Mike Aquilina [Our
Sunday Visitor] – Learn how the Mass of the Early
Church is the same Mass we celebrate today.
H, A, ✠

*Where We Got the Bible: Our Debt to the Catholic
Church* by Rev. Henry G. Graham – The Catholic
Church is a "Bible church" and the Bible is a Catholic
book.
H, A, ✠

The First Christians: The Acts of the Apostles by
Marigold Hunt [Sophia] – Originally published in

History

1953, reissued with new illustrations in 2004, this is a nice read aloud. The author does a good job motivating the reader to go to the Bible to learn more about the Early Church and the Apostles.

G, M, ✠

The Ides of April **(Young Adult Historical Bookshelf)** by Mary Ray [Bethlehem] – Set in Rome, 62 AD, this is a history mystery, which takes you on quite the adventure. The main character is a seventeen-year-old slave who looks to save himself, his mother, and other household slaves from death when their master, a prominent senator, is murdered.

II, ✠

Beyond the Desert Gate **(Young Adult Historical Bookshelf)** by Mary Ray [Bethlehem] – This is the sequel to *The Ides of April* and takes place in 70 AD Palestine.

H, ✠

Saint Paul (?-67)

The Silver Chalice by Thomas Costain – I gave this novel as a gift to a 15-year old and she now tells all her friends this is the best book ever written. It is a great way to explore Luke, Paul, and the other apostles as they worked to build Christ's Church.

H, A

Saint Paul the Apostle: The Story of the Apostle to the Gentiles by Mary Fabyan Windeatt [TAN] – This inspiring story will introduce your children to the trials Paul endured to bring Christianity to the world. Makes a nice read aloud.

G, M, ✠

History

St. Peter (?-64)
Nero (37-68)

City of the Golden House by Madeleine Polland [Hillside Education] – A crippled Roman boy and his slave become a part of the Christian underground during the time of Nero.
M, H, ✠

The Man Who Never Died: The Life and Adventures of St. Peter, the First Pope by Rev. Gerald T. Brennan [Sophia] – The story of the first pope is not a dull one. This is a great book to introduce children to Peter.
G, M , ✠

Mount Vesuvius Buries Pompeii (79)

Pompeii . . . Buried Alive (Step-Into-Reading, Step 4) by Edith Kunhardt – The eruption of Mt. Vesuvius and its aftermath is described in detail. Very interesting to children, however it may be too much for a sensitive child.
G

Word to Caesar (Hillside Education Study Guide) by Geoffrey Trease [Hillside] – Novel about Imperial Rome set in 117. The orphaned son of a Roman soldier travels to escape war and is rescued by the poet Severus. Study questions are included at the end of each chapter.
M, ✠

The Eagle of the Ninth by Rosemary Sutcliff – It's the year 125 and a young Roman centurion must recover the Ninth Legion's missing symbol of honor, the Eagle Standard, which mysteriously disappeared under his father's command.
H

The Silver Branch by Rosemary Sutcliff – Sequel to *The Eagle of the Ninth*, it's the year 250 when Roman rule

is waning. Two cousins join forces with the lost Ninth Legion to fight a tyrannical British emperor.
H

St. Valentine (?-270)

Saint Valentine by Robert Sabuda – The illustrations are mosaics of hand-painted, marbleized paper. They almost look like icons. The story is nicely told, and it's a delight to read on St. Valentine's Day.
P, G

Diocletian (245-313)

Fabiola, or the Church of the Catacombs by Cardinal Wiseman [Lepanto] – Originally published in 1886, this is the story of the Christian martyrs under Diocletian. Martyrs such as Sts. Sebastian, Agnes, and Tarcisius.
H, A, ✠

St. Athanasius (c.297-373), Egypt

Saint Athanasius by F.A. Forbes [TAN] – Originally published in 1919, this book is fairly easy to read. It chronicles the life of Saint Athanasius who was the Bishop of Alexandria and a Doctor of the Church.
M, H, ✠

St. Monica (332-387), North Africa and Rome
St. Augustine (354-430)

Confessions by Saint Augustine – This is Augustine's autobiography. It's a beautiful story, which should be on every Christian's reading list.
H, A, ✠

City of God by Saint Augustine – Augustine's monumental work of religion, history, and philosophy.
H, A, ✠

History

The Restless Flame by Louis de Wohl [Ignatius] – This historical fiction book tells the story of St. Augustine in a very engaging way. Be forewarned: Augustine's womanizing before his conversion is included, though not in great detail.
H, A, ✠

St. Monica: Model of Christian Mothers by F.A. Forbes [TAN] – You can buy this book individually or as a seven-book set of Forbes' saint biographies.
M, H, ✠

St. Patrick (385-461), England and Ireland

Patrick: Patron Saint of Ireland by Tomie de Paola – de Paola integrates beautifulCeltic design into his illustrations. He presents both the historical and legendary Patrick.
P, G, ✠

St. Nicholas (c. fourth century), Turkey

Saint Nicholas: The Wonder Worker by Anne Neuberger [Our Sunday Visitor] – Tells the story of the historical St. Nicholas, as well as the legends that developed about him around the world.
M, ✠

The Lantern Bearers by Rosemary Sutcliff – It's 450 in Britain, and Aquila, a young legionnaire, decides not to leave Britain with the last of the Roman Auxiliaries. His loyalty lies with Britain, so he joins the forces of the Roman-British leader and fights against the Saxon hordes.
H

Between the Forest and the Hills (**Adventure Library**) by Ann Lawrence [Bethlehem] – Billed as historical

fantasy, this is an enjoyable story about the last days
of the Roman Empire.

H, ✠

China / Asia

*The Samurai and the Tea: A Legacy of Japan's Early
Christians* by Cathy Brueggemann-Beil [Imprint] –
This story centers on the Japanese tea ceremony. A
Japanese-American boy travels back in time to learn
about Catholic martyrs and how the faith survived in
Japan.

H, A, ✠

Ancient China (**DK Eyewitness**) – The New York Times
describes this series as "a mini museum between the
covers of a book." This title explores the history of the
Chinese empire and its culture.

G, M

Russia (**DK Eyewitness**) – In-depth photo essay of Russia
from ancient to modern times.

G, M

*Made in China: Ideas and Inventions from Ancient
China* by Suzanne Williams – This book could be tied
into a science unit study on the greatest inventions
throughout history. Begins in 1700 BC and ends in the
sixteenth century.

G, M

Growing Up in Ancient China by Ken Teague – Written
from a child's perspective, this book teaches about
Ancient China's customs, education, family life, food,
and more.

G

The Empty Pot by Demi – A lovely story teaching honesty
is the best policy. A nice way to introduce Chinese
culture to little ones.

P, G

The Story of Noodles by Ying Chang Compestine, illustrated by Yong Sheng Xuan – A funny story about the
mischievous Kang brothers who stumble upon the
invention of noodles. If you like this story, check out
Compestine's other picture books about China.
P, G

The Empress and the Silkworm by Lily Toy Hong – Takes
place in 2640 BC and tells the legend of how silk was
discovered. Includes background information at the
end including how the secret of silk was kept hidden
for 3,000 years.
P, G

Gautama Buddha (540-483 BC)

Buddha by Demi – Demi is a Buddhist and so this book is
written from that world-view. Covering both legend
and facts, this picture book will give you the opportunity to talk to children about other religions.
. P, G

King Cheng, Ch'in Dynasty (221-206 BC)
The Great Wall of China

The Great Wall of China by Leonard Everett Fisher –
Fact-filled picture book about the building of one of
the seven wonders of the world.
G

The Silk Route (c.100 BC-500 AD)

The Silk Route: 7,000 Miles of History by John S. Major
– Learning about the Silk Road is an important part of
understanding Chinese history and trade.
G

Paper Invented (c. 100)

The Story of Paper by Ying Chang Compestine – The Kang brothers are back and this time they stumble upon the invention of paper.
P, G

Attila the Hun (?-453)

The Darkness and the Dawn, A Novel by Thomas Costain – Costain, a favorite novelist, tells the story of Attila the Hun.
H, A

All Men Are Brothers / Shui Hu Chuan by Shi Nai'an, translated by Pearl Buck – This classic Chinese novel takes place in the twelfth century. Tells the story of a band of patriots who struggle to help the emperor get rid of the prime minister. Look for parallels to Robin Hood, written a hundred years later.
A

The Black Rose by Thomas Costain – Takes place around 1273. Walter of Gurnie is forced to flee Oxford for his part in the university riots. He travels to China, leaving behind the love of his life. The plot thickens when he returns to England.
H, A

Marco Polo (1254-1324)

Travels by Marco Polo – Polo's personal telling of his journey to the Far East and back. A great find if you're into primary documents.
H, A

St. Francis Xavier (1506-1552)

Set All Afire: A Story About St. Francis Xavier by Louis de Wohl [Ignatius] – St. Ignatius directed St. Francis to "set all afire" in the Orient. His is a captivating story, which is both historically intriguing and spiritually uplifting.

H, A, ✠

***St. Francis of the Seven Seas* (Vision Book)** by Alfred J. Nevins, MM [Ignatius] – This great missionary spread the faith to the Far East, even in the face of grave danger.

M, H, ✠

The Samurai's Tale by Erik Christian Haugard – I enjoyed this novel set in turbulent sixteenth century Japan. The hero's family is murdered and he is taken as a servant. He goes from being a simple servant boy to a samurai.

H, A

King Mongkut of Siam (1804-1868), Thailand

Anna and the King of Siam by Margaret Landon – *The King and I* was based on this book, written more than sixty years ago. Blending fact and fiction, it tells the story of an Englishwoman who becomes governess to the children of King Mongkut of Siam in the 1860's.

H, A

Kim by Rudyard Kipling – Takes place after the Indian uprising in 1858. The hero is an orphaned boy of Irish and Indian descent. The reader gets an insider's view to India through Kim's adventure.

H, A

The Man Who Would be King and Other Short Stories by Rudyard Kipling – Contains five of Kipling's best short stories, taking place in 1885-1888 India.

H, A

Young Fu of the Upper Yangtze by Elizabeth F. Lewis –
Might be described as a rags-to-riches story. Young Fu
is a country boy who is apprenticed to a master cop-
persmith during the turbulent 1920's in China.
M, H

The Good Earth by Pearl Buck – A Pulitzer Prize winner,
this book gives the reader a peek into the last days of
emperors and the social upheavals that took place during that time. Also presents the opportunity to discuss
whether wealth brings happiness and the moral decay
that occurs when a person takes their first deceitful
step. Parents should read before giving to a student.
H, A, *

Homesick: My Own Story by Jean Fritz – This autobiographical story takes place in the mid-1920's. Fritz
was born to American parents in China and lived there
until she was twelve.
M

World War II (1939-1945)
Dropping of the Atomic Bomb (Aug. 6, 1945), Japan
Hiroshima by John Hersey – This true recounting of
Hiroshima was first written in 1946 for New Yorker
magazine. The final chapter wasn't written until 1985
when Hersey returned to Hiroshima and revisited six
of the people he had interviewed almost forty years
earlier.
H, A

The House of Sixty Fathers by Meindert DeJong, illustrated by Maurice Sendak – Takes place shortly after the
Japanese invasion of China. A young boy journeys
across Japanese-occupied land to find his family and
then safety with the American troops.
G

History

Up Periscope by Robb White – Based on a true story. The famous movie of the same title is based on this children's book.
G

Crow Boy by Taro Yashimo – Chibi is an outcast in his Japanese village and school. The moral at the end is very touching.
P, G

Vikings

The Children of Odin: The Book of Northern Myths by Padraic Colum – An excellent retelling of the Norse sagas about Odin, Freya, Thor, Loki, and other gods and goddesses who the Vikings believed lived in Asgard before the dawn of time.
M, H

D'Aulaires' Book of Norse Myths by Ingri and Edgar d'Aulaire – This is a beautifully illustrated introduction to Norse myths.
M

Viking (DK Eyewitness) – The same two-page layout with great photos and interesting facts as all the titles in this series. I sometimes use this series for writing prompts or copywork. This title explores the world of the Vikings.
G, M

Beowulf the Warrior by Ian Serraillier [Bethlehem] – Set in 500 Denmark, the mighty and brave Beowulf defeats the evil Grendel and his mother. A classic rewritten for children.
M, H, ✠

Beorn the Proud by Madelaine Polland [Bethlehem] – Takes place c. 800 in Iceland and Denmark. Beorn is the arrogant young son of a Viking chieftain who captures a Christian girl from Ireland, and takes her as a slave. The contrast between the One True God and the multiple Norse gods is clear.

M, H, ✠

Leif Erikson (975-1020)

Leif the Lucky by Ingri and Edgar d'Aulaire – Can also be tied into American history along with the story of Brendan the Navigator. This is the tale of a young explorer who finds his way to Newfoundland and who is also converted to Christianity.

G, M

The Story of Rolf & the Viking Bow by Allen French [Bethlehem] – Takes place c. 1000 Iceland. Rolf is a young bowman set on avenging his father's death. He faces many dangers as he seeks to bring justice to his father's murderers.

M, H, ✠

Sword of Clontarf by Charles Brady [Hillside Education] – Takes place in 1014 Iceland and Ireland. A great adventure story of an Icelandic boy who, when his father is murdered, must make a dangerous trip to Ireland. It is a story of courage, compassion, and integrity. Hillside offers an accompanying study guide.

M, ✠

Kristin Lavransdatter Series by Sigrid Undset – Takes place in fourteenth century Norway. Kristin Lavransdatter is not perfect. Spirited and head strong, she gives into forbidden love, pays the consequences, and learns from her mistakes. This is a beautiful story about spiritual growth and family, as well as a story that is faithful to history. Parents should read before giving to their student.

H, A, ✠, *

Africa

2000 Years of Christianity in Africa: An African Church History by John Baur [Paulines Africa] – A history of the Church in Africa, from the first century to recent times.

H, A, ✠

Saints of Africa by Vincent O'Malley, C.M. [Our Sunday Visitor] – A compilation of biographies for nearly ninety African saints. Can be used as a brief history of the Catholic Church in Africa.

H, A, ✠

Not Out of Africa: How Afrocentrism Became an Excuse to Teach Myth As History by Mary Lefkowitz – For the older student and parent. Examines the Afrocentric view of history.

H, A

Africa **(DK Eyewitness)** – Photo essay of Africa. Just an overview since it would be impossible to study this vast continent in one slender book.

G, M

Mohammed (570-632)

Inside Islam: A Guide for Catholics: 100 Questions and Answers by Daniel Ali and Robert Spencer [Ascension] – It's important in today's world for Americans to understand the history and culture of Islam. This book is in an easy-to-read, question and answer format.

H, A, ✠

King of the Wind by Marguerite Henry – This is a great book for children who love horse stories. The boy and his horse begin in 1700's Morocco, travel to the royal

courts of France, and in the end to the stately homes
of England.
M

King Solomon's Mines by H. Rider Haggard – Taking
place in the 1880's, this is a thrilling story about an
elephant hunter's safari deep into Africa and the
search for legendary treasure mines.
H, A

St. Charles Lwanga (?-1886), Uganda
Ugandan Martyrs (1885-1887)

African Holocaust: The Story of the Uganda Martyrs by
J.F. Faupel, MHM [Paulines Africa] – A documented
account of the Uganda Martyrs.
H, A, ✠

King Leopold II (1835-1909), Belgium and Congo

King Leopold's Ghost by Joseph Conrad – Chronicles
King Leopold II's rule of terror over the Congo. It is a
horrifying story of mine slave labor, cruel dismember-
ment, and mass murder.
H, A, *

Heart of Darkness and Other Tales by Joseph Conrad
Historical fiction set in 1890's Congo during the
height of Leopold's terror.
H, A

Bl. Isidore Bakanja (1887-1909), Congo and Zaire

Bakanja by Aldo Falconi, SSP [Pauline] – Blessed
Bakanja Isidore was martyred for teaching the
Catholic faith.
M, ✠

St. Josephine Bakhita (1869-1947), Sudan
Bakhita: From Slavery to Sanctity [Pauline] – St.
  Josephine is a favorite saint. She is a beautiful exam-
  ple to all of us, no matter the color of our skin, of true
  Christian humility and service.
  M, ✠

Cry, the Beloved Country by Alan Paton – Story of a Zulu
  pastor and his son, set in the troubled 1940's South
  Africa.
  H, A

Early Middle Ages – Europe – 500 to 1000
*How the Irish Saved Civilization: The Untold Story of
  Ireland's Heroic Role from the Fall of Rome to the
  Rise of Medieval Europe* by Thomas Cahill – The
  monks and scribes of Ireland laboriously preserved the
  literary classics of the West as Europe was being pil-
  laged by the Barbarians.
  A
*Religion and the Rise of Western Culture: The Classic
  Study of Medieval Civilization* by Christopher
  Dawson – This is a serious study that looks at the
  impact of religion on history, beginning with the fall
  of Rome and ending with the Renaissance. This is an
  academic book best left for the university student or
  knowledgeable adult.
  A
Europe and the Faith by Hilaire Belloc [TAN] – Belloc
  writes it was the Catholic Church that made Europe.
  H, A, ✠
The Building of Christendom (**History of Christendom,
  vol. 2)** by Warren H. Carroll [Christendom] – This
  series is a comprehensive history by orthodox Catholic

professor Warren Carroll. This volume covers 324 to 1100.

H, A, ✠

King Arthur (c. 537), England

Sir Gawain and the Green Knight by unknown, translated by J. R. R. Tolkein – This narrative poem takes the reader back to the days of chivalry, knights, and holy quests.
M, H

King Arthur by Howard Pyle – Pyle is a favorite author and his version of King Arthur is superior.
M, H

The Sword in the Tree by Clyde Robert Bulla – An eleven-year-old boy saves the day in King Arthur's court.
G

St. Benedict (480-547), Italy

Citadel of God by Louis de Wohl [Ignatius] – A novel set during the chaotic days of the Barbarians, with St. Benedict at the center.
H, A, ✠

Saint Benedict: The Story of the Father of the Western Monks by Mary Fabyan Windeatt [TAN] – Also available from Ignatius Press as part of the Vision Book Series. St. Benedict is essential in understanding the Early Middle Ages.
M, ✠

St. Brendan (484-577), Ireland

The Brendan Voyage: Across the Atlantic in a Leather Boat by Timothy Severin – The author took an extraordinary voyage with a small crew by recreating St. Brendan's journey from Ireland to America. They used only materials that would have been available to the Irish saint.

H, A

Brendan the Navigator: A History Mystery About the Discovery of America by Jean Fritz – If you ask children in Ireland who discovered America, they probably will not answer Columbus or the Vikings, but "St. Brendan the Navigator, of course!" Keep in mind when reading this book that even though it's written about a saint, it's written from a secular world view.

G

St. Colomba (521-597), Ireland and Scotland

Fingal's Quest by Madeleine A. Polland [Lepanto] – Fingal is a poor, fatherless boy who becomes a student in an Irish monastery. He stows away to follow his teacher Colomba when he leaves to evangelize Europe. Also published by Savio.

M, H, ✠

The Man Who Loved Books by Jean Fritz – Biography of the Irish Saint Columba who not only loved books, but was a missionary to Scotland.

G

Gregory, Bishop of Tours (573-594)

The History of the Franks by Gregory of Tours – Surprisingly, this history is told in a gossipy tone. Gregory relates the story of the founding of France, Christianity's impact, royal families, and more.

H, A, ✠

St. Augustine of Canterbury (?-604), Rome and England

Augustine Comes to Kent (Living History Library) by Barbara Willard [Bethlehem] – A nice read aloud, tells

the story of a young boy who travels with St.
Augustine to bring Christianity to England.
M, ✠

St. Bede the Scholar (673-735), England
Ecclesiastical History of the English People by St. Bede –
Read the actual words of this unassuming abbot, who
writes his history through the lens of the Church. A
must read for the English history scholar.
H, A, ✠

Charlemagne (768-814)
Two Lives of Charlemagne by Einhard and Notker the
Stammerer – The one life of Charlemagne written by
two historians of his own day.
H, A
Son of Charlemagne (**Living History Library**) by
Barbara Willard [Bethlehem] – Learn about
Charlemagne (Charles the Great) through the life of
his eldest son. Enjoyable read.
G, M, ✠

Feudalism
Castle by David Macaulay – Extremely detailed text and
drawings of the building of a thirteenth century castle
in Wales.
G, M, H
Medieval Life (**DK Eyewitness**) – An overview of the
Middle Ages and everyday life.
G, M
Knight (**DK Eyewitness**) – Photo essay of the life and
times of Medieval knights. Learn about armor,
weapons, jousts, and more.
G, M

Castle (**DK Eyewitness**) – An informative guide to the European castles of the Medieval and Renaissance periods.

G, M

Design Your Own Coat of Arms: An Introduction to Heraldry by Rosemary Chorzempa – My children love this book. Even after our Medieval studies came to an end, they continued to create their own coat of arms. The book also includes John Paul II's coat of arms as a modern example of heraldry.

G, M, H

Grimm's Fairy Tales – Fairy tales are not history, but they do give a feel for the era in which they were written. We read one fairy tale a week when studying the Middle Ages. It's a fun diversion, but still beneficial.

G, M, H

King Alfred the Great (849-901), England

Ballad of the White Horse by G. K. Chesterton [Ignatius] – Chesterton's epic poem, considered by many to be his best work. Explores the Danish invasion of England and King Alfred's courageous efforts to fight back the pagan invaders. He relied heavily on the help of Mary to defend his country's Christian lands. Memorable passages, which will especially hold the interest of boys.

H, A, ✠

The Little Duke (**Knights and Ladies**) by Charlotte Yonge [Lepanto] – Takes place in 943 France and is about the childhood of Richard the Fearless, Duke of Normandy.

M, H, ✠

High Middle Ages – Europe – 1000 to 1300

The Glory of Christendom **(History of Christendom, vol. 3)** by Warren H. Carroll [Christendom] – The third of four books in this series. Covers the period from 1100 to 1517 AD.

H, A, ✠

King Harold II (1022-1066), England

Battle of Hastings (1066), England

The King's Shadow by Elizabeth Alden – A young Welsh orphan, disfigured by his father's murderer, eventually finds himself the foster son of England's last Saxon king – Harold II. The story comes to a head at the Battle of Hastings and Harold's death.

M, H

William the Conqueror (1027-1087), France and England

William the Conqueror by Hilaire Belloc [TAN] – Explores William's Catholicism and its impact on England.

H, A, ✠

St Anselm (1033-1109)

Anselm's Proslogion – Anselm's proof, or argument, of God's existence. Look for an edition with notes and the prayers of St. Anselm. You can also search the Internet to download for free.

H, A, ✠

The First Crusade (1095-1099)

The Crusades by Hilaire Belloc [TAN] – Why did the Crusades initially succeed but ultimately fail? Belloc explains it all through the lens of the Catholic Church.

H, A, ✠

Chronicles of the Crusades by Geoffroy deVillehardouin and Jean deJoinville – Two separate accounts of the Crusades written by soldiers who participated in the Crusades themselves. DeVillehardouin's account is of the Fourth Crusade and the conquest of Constantinople. DeJoinville's account is of the Sixth and Seventh Crusades, concentrating on St. Louis.
H, A

The Blue Gonfalon: At the First Crusade by Margaret Ann Hubbard [Lepanto] – A French peasant boy dreams of knighthood. It looks like it may come true when he heads to Palestine as a squire.
M, H, ✠

The Red Keep: A Story of Burgundy in 1165 (**Adventure Library**) by Allen French [Bethlehem] – A young squire takes on the task of overcoming a pair of robber barons who pillage and terrorize the local countryside.
M, H, ✠

St. Thomas Becket (1118-1170), England
King Henry II (1154-1189), England
Murder in the Cathedral by T. S. Elliot – Known as a "poetic drama," this short read (96 pages) is a 1935 play written in verse. Shakespearian in style, symbolism and imagery abounds. Deals more with Becket's inner conflict with his conscience than with his conflict (over judicial authority in church matters) with Henry II.
H, A, ✠

If All the Swords In England (**Living History Library**) by Barbara Willard [Bethlehem] – History is revealed through the story of twin brothers separated after the tragic deaths of their parents. The story picks up in

1170 with one brother in the service of King Henry II
and the other in the service of Archbishop Becket.
M, H, ✠

***The Hidden Treasure of Glaston* (Living History
Library)** by Eleanore Jewitt [Bethlehem] – Takes
place the year following Beckett's murder. A lame boy,
whose knight father has been exiled, searches for
relics of King Arthur. A great adventure to read aloud.
M, ✠

**King Richard the Lion Hearted (1157-1199), England
Saladin (c. 1137-1193), Palestine
Third Crusade (1189-1192)**

The Talisman by Sir Walter Scott – Set in the deserts of
Palestine with King Richard and his Crusaders. Has
everything you need for adventure: sultans, knights,
kings, Nubian slaves, duals, conspiracies, and more.
H, A

Ivanhoe by Sir Walter Scott [Lepanto] – While King
Richard is off fighting in the Crusades, Prince John
takes advantage of his brother's absence, plotting to
take over the throne. Richard returns and seeks the
help of a courageous soldier: Wilfred of Ivanhoe.
H, A

**King John (1167-1216), England
The Magna Carta (1215), England**

King John by William Shakespeare – John's questionable
rise to the throne, murder, revenge, a doting mother
(Eleanor of Aquitaine), what more could you ask for?
H, A

The Magna Charta by James Daugherty – The deceit and
corruption of King John pushed the people to create a
document to secure their freedom and bring justice.

We skipped the last chapter on the U.N., which is outdated.

M, H

The Merry Adventures of Robin Hood by Howard Pyle –
Pyle's version of Robin Hood is by far the best. The
language is far from modern, but my children had no
trouble rising to the occasion.

M, H

The Lost Baron: A Story of England in the Year 1200
(Adventure Library) by Allen French [Bethlehem] –
An adventure, which will be especially enjoyed by
boys. Filled with mystery, conniving relatives, squires,
deceit, and secret passages.

M, H, ✠

Fifth Crusade (1218)

Big John's Secret **(Living History Library)** by Eleanore
M. Jewett [Bethlehem] – A young squire sets off with
the Crusaders, hoping to find his lost father. He cross-
es paths with St. Francis of Assisi and becomes a part
of history.

M, ✠

St. Dominic (1170-1221), Spain

St. Dominic and the Rosary **(Vision Book)** by Catherine
Beebe [Ignatius] – As an educator, I appreciate the
importance placed in this book on the importance of
receiving a solid education. This is a well-written,
enjoyable story.

M, H, ✠

*St. Dominic: Preacher of the Rosary and Founder of the
Dominican Order* by Mary Fabyan Windeatt [TAN] –
St. Dominic was given the Holy Rosary by the
Blessed Mother. He also defeated heresy, triumphed
over Satan, raised the dead, and started the

Dominicans. A great story.

G, M, ✠

St. Francis of Assisi (1181-1226), Italy
St. Clare (1194-1253), Italy

The Joyful Beggar: St. Francis of Assisi by Louis de
    Wohl [Ignatius] – This is a high quality historical fic-
    tion, bringing understanding of the times as well as the
    life of St. Francis.

    H, A, ✠

St. Francis of Assisi by G. K. Chesterton [Ignatius] – The
    story of St. Francis has been told many times, but
    Chesterton, who heard the story at his father's knee,
    had a life-long love for this saint. Chesterton under-
    stood the saint as a holy fool, a simple poor beggar,
    and as an ascetic bound for heaven. A fascinating and
    romantic look at the holy dreamer of Assisi.

    H, A, ✠

Francis and Clare: Saints of Assisi **(Vision Book)** by
    Helen Walker Homan [Ignatius] – Not only informa-
    tive but humorous, this narrative brings Francis and
    Clare alive.

    M, H, ✠

Saint Francis Assisi: Gentle Revolutionary **(Encounter
    the Saints)** by Mary Emmanuel Alves, FSP [Pauline]
    – This series is made up of easy-to-read and inexpen-
    sive chapter books. Learn how the rich merchant's son
    came to be born in a stable and went on to dedicate his
    life to poverty and to God.

    G, M, ✠

Francis by Mother Mary Francis, PCC [Catholic Heritage
    Curricula] – Mother Mary Francis was a talented sto-
    ryteller and the illustrations by the Poor Clare nuns are
    very nice.

    G, ✠

History

Francis: The Poor Man of Assisi by Tomie dePaola –
Colorful, entertaining, and historical. Beautiful lesson
in simplicity.

G, ✠

St. Anthony of Padua (1195-1231), Italy and Portugal

St. Anthony and the Christ Child **(Vision Book)** by Helen
Walker Homan [Ignatius] – Little is known about St.
Anthony's life, so a large chunk of this story comes
from the author's imagination.

M, ✠

Saint Anthony of Padua: Fire and Light **(Encounter the
Saints)** by Margaret Charles Kerry, FSP and Mary
Elizabeth Tebo, FSP [Pauline] – Learn why St.
Anthony is the patron of lost items.

G, M, ✠

St. Elizabeth of Hungary (1207-1231), Hungary

St. Elizabeth's Three Crowns **(Vision Book**) by Blanche
Thompson [Ignatius] – St. Elizabeth was a queen,
though she longed for a life of poverty. She was a
Third Order Franciscan. She was very generous with
her wealth and canonized just four years after her
death.

M, H, ✠

St. Hyacinth (1185-1257), Poland

*Saint Hyacinth of Poland: The Story of the Apostle of the
North* by Mary Fabyan Windeatt [TAN] – St.
Hyacinth was a Dominican missionary to Lithuania,
Russia, and Poland. Many of his adventures are shared
in this book.

M, ✠

Guilds and Trades

Cathedral: The Story of Its Construction by David
  Macaulay – The cathedral in this book is fictional,
  based on the construction of several Medieval cathe-
  drals. Gives great insight into all the details of building a cathedral from its inception to its completion.
  You'll need to explain to children the author makes a
  mistake in stating that relics were worshipped.
  G, M, H

St. Thomas Aquinas (1225-1274), Italy

The Quiet Light by Louis de Wohl [Ignatius] – It is said
  the theme of *The Quiet Light* was suggested to de
  Wohl in a private audience with Pope Pius XII. This
  novelization of St. Thomas Aquinas' life also details
  thirteenth century life in Europe.
  H, A, ✠

St. Thomas Aquinas: The Dumb Ox by G. K. Chesterton
  [Ignatius] – Almost legendary, Chesterton sent his sec-
  retary for a stack of books on St. Thomas. Chesterton
  placed his hand on the stack and then proceeded to
  write this book, which according to one famous
  Thomist scholar, is the best book on Thomas ever.
  H, A, ✠

*Praying in the Presence of Our Lord: With St. Thomas
  Aquinas* by Mike Aquilina [Our Sunday Visitor] –
  Aquinas wrote beautiful hymns to be prayed before
  the Blessed Sacrament. This book includes those
  hymns in both the original Latin and English. One day,
  I would love to build a unit study around this book. I
  could easily tie in Latin, poetry, theology, and history.
  M, H, A, ✠

St. Thomas Aquinas and the Preaching Beggars (**Vision
  Book**) by Fr. Brendan Larnen and Milton Lomask
  [Ignatius] – How St. Thomas came to be called the

"Dumb Ox" in school, and then went on to become one of the most brilliant minds in the Church.
M, H, ✠

St. Thomas Aquinas: The Story of the Dumb Ox by Mary Fabyan Windeatt [TAN] – When we think of St. Thomas, we usually think about his Summa and not his dramatic escape from a castle tower. This book brings St. Thomas alive for children.
G, M, ✠

Adam of the Road by Elizabeth Gray – A young boy travels the roads of 1294 England in search of his minstrel father and his stolen cocker spaniel.
M, H

Late Middle Ages – Europe – 1300 to 1400

A Medieval Feast by Aliki – This picture book is about all that went into a great feast prepared for visiting royalty, c.1400. I used this book, along with authentic recipes found on the Internet, with my history co-op when we prepared our own Medieval feast. The illustrations were inspired by actual medieval tapestries.
P, G

Bl. Imelda Lambertini (1322-1333), Italy

Patron Saint of First Communicants: The Story of Blessed Imelda Lambertini by Mary Fabyan Windeatt [TAN] – Bl. Imelda dies in ecstasy when she takes her First Holy Communion, so may not be appropriate for all children. However, my children loved her story and were impressed by Imelda's love for Jesus in the Eucharist.
G, M, ✠

Hundred Year's War (1327-1453)
The Black Death (1348-1352)

The Door in the Wall by Marguerite DeAngeli – Set in
fourteenth century England, tells the story of a boy
who survives the plague. Left crippled, his dreams of
becoming a knight are dashed. Even so, he is able to
save the day when the castle is attacked.
G, M

The Gauntlet **(Knights and Ladies)** by Ronald Welch
[Lepanto]   A boy wandering through castle ruins
finds himself transported back to the fourteenth century.
M, ✠

King Edward III (1312-1377), England
The Lances of Lynwood **(Knights and Ladies)** by
Charlotte M. Yonge [Lepanto] – A heroic act in battle
wins a young Eustace the favor of the Prince of Wales
and the knighthood.
M, H, ✠

St. Catherine of Siena (1347-1380), Italy
*Lay Siege to Heaven: A Novel About St. Catherine of
Siena* by Louis de Wohl [Ignatius] – This author has a
way of bringing the saints alive for his readers. Both
my teens and I love the de Wohl novels. I think high
school students will be drawn to St. Catherine through
this story.
H, A, ✠

Saint Catherine of Siena by F. A. Forbes [TAN] – An
incredible story of a girl born to wealth during troubled times. Tells of St. Catherine's visions, devotion to
prayer, obedience, and humility.
M, H, ✠

St. Catherine of Siena: The Story of the Girl Who Saw Saints in the Sky by Mary Fabyan Windeatt [TAN] – It was St. Catherine who brought the pope back to Rome from France and helped him upon his return. This is a great story of a woman who went on to become a Doctor of the Church.
G, M, ✠

Henry IV (1367-1413), England

Men of Iron by Howard Pyle [Lepanto] – This great story takes place late in King Henry IV's reign. A young boy helps to clear his father's name when he is wrongly accused of treason.
M, H

Thomas a Kempis (1379-1471), Germany and Netherlands

Imitation of Christ [Ignatius] - This is the second most widely read spiritual work after the Bible.
H, A, ✠

Renaissance – Europe – 1400 to 1700

The Cleaving of Christendom (History of Christendom, vol. 4) by Warren Carroll [Christendom] – The final book of the series, this one covers 1517 to 1661.
H, A, ✠

Sun Slower, Sun Faster (Living History Library) by Meriol Trevor [Bethlehem] – I'm not a big fan of time travel books, but I enjoyed this one. Two 1950's children go back to varying times in history, in and around Bristol, England.
M, H, ✠

Otto of the Silver Hand by Howard Pyle – Written in 1888 but still loved by modern children. Set in c. 1400 Germany, the gentle Otto, raised by monks, is kid-

napped and mutilated by a rival family. Otto's strong
character prevails. A must read.

M, H

St. Joan of Arc (1412-1431), France

Personal Recollections of Joan of Arc by Mark Twain
[Ignatius] – A fantastic and readable book using historically accurate data. Mark Twain worked for twelve
years on this epic and considered it his best work.

H, A

Joan of Arc by Hilaire Belloc [Neumann] – This is a slim,
yet enjoyable, biography.

H, A, ✠

Saint Joan: The Girl Soldier (**Vision Book**) by Louis de
Wohl [Ignatius] – de Wohl, known as a novelist,
applies his extraordinary skill to this children's book.
He delves into the source of Joan's heroism – her deep
love for her Creator.

M, H, ✠

Saint Joan of Arc: God's Soldier (**Encounter the Saints**)
by Susan Helen Walace FSP [Pauline] – This is a very
nice series of books, which can be purchased individually or as a complete set from Pauline.

G, M, ✠

The Trumpeter of Krakow by Eric P. Kelly – Set in 1461
Poland, this story is built around two Polish legends.
The first is one of a trumpeter who, in keeping his
oath (as a trumpeter), is killed by the invading Tartars
earlier in 1241. The other legend involves a treasure
entrusted to the family of this story – The Great
Tarnov Crystal. It all comes to a great end, after a lot
of exciting twists and turns.

M, H

Johann Gutenburg (1391-1468), Germany
Fine Print: A Story about Johann Gutenberg by Joann J.
    Burch – The printing press was the modern technology
    of Gutenberg's day. Its invention has an important
    place in history. Learn how Gutenberg's tenacity
    brought it all about.
    G. M

King Richard III (1453-1485), England
Richard the Third by Paul Kendall – Well-researched
    biography. Might be read alongside Shakespeare's
    Richard III to separate fact from fiction in the Bard's
    play.
    H, A

The War of the Roses (1455-1485), England
The Black Arrow by Robert Louis Stevenson – Classic
    book set in the reign of Henry VI during the War of
    the Roses. The language is a bit archaic, but can be
    understood in context. A great story.
    H, A
Grisly Grisell: A Tale of the War of the Roses **(Knights
    and Ladies)** by Charlotte Yonge [Lepanto] – Story of
    a beautiful girl, Grisell, who is left disfigured after a
    terrible accident. With the War of the Roses raging, the
    mettle of the book's characters is tested.
    M, H, ✠

King Ferdinand V (1452-1516), Spain
Queen Isabella I (1451-1504), Spain
Isabel of Spain: The Catholic Queen by Warren H.
    Carroll [Christendom] – A scholarly biography of one
    of the most powerful women in history.
    H, A, ✠

Spanish Inquisition (1478)

Characters of the Inquisition by William Thomas Walsh
  [TAN] – Misconceptions abound about the Spanish
  Inquisition. This book traces the lives of the prominent
  figures of the Inquisition and the history of past inqui-
  sitions. Many false accusations against the Church are
  put to rest.
  H, A, ✠

Christopher Columbus (1451-1506), Italy and Spain Discovers America (1492)

The Log of Christopher Columbus' First Voyage – A
  great primary source: Columbus' actual ship log.
  G, M, H

Christopher Columbus by Ingri and Edgar d'Aulaire – I
  love the d'Aulaire books, which are being republished
  by Beautiful Feet. They are beautifully illustrated and
  packed full of interesting history.
  G, M

*Where Do You Think You're Going Christopher
  Columbus?* by Jean Fritz – Like many of Fritz's
  books, this is a colorful, fun, easy read.
  G

The Story of Columbus (DK Beginner Reader) by Anita
  Garneri – A simple picture book to introduce children
  to Christopher Columbus.
  P, G

St. John Fisher (1469-1535), England

Saint John Fisher by Michael Davies [Neumann] – St.
  John Fisher was the confessor to Lady Margaret
  Beaufort, mother of King Henry VII, as well as tutor
  to Prince Henry. Prince Henry grew up to be Henry
  VIII and executed St. John Fisher.
  M, H, ✠

History

Martin Luther (1483-1546), Germany
95 Theses (1517)
Characters of the Reformation by Hilaire Belloc [TAN] –
Analyzes the lives of the main characters of the
Protestant Reformation.
H, A, ✠
Roots of the Reformation by Karl Adam [Coming Home
Network] – A Catholic classic. Extremely balanced
view of both sides of the issue.
H, A, ✠

St. Thomas More (1478-1536), England
NF *A Man for All Seasons* by Robert Bolt – The famous
movie, one of my favorites, was based on this book.
H, A
St. Thomas More of London (**Vision Book**) by Elizabeth
Ince [Ignatius] – St. Thomas was martyred by King
Henry VIII for his loyalty to Rome and his refusal to
see Henry as head of the Catholic Church in England.
The author of this Vision Book is a descendant of St.
Thomas More.
M, H, ✠

King Henry VIII (1491-1547), England
The King's Achievement by Hugh Benson [Neumann] –
Historical novel about how people remained faithful to
the Church, even amidst Henry VIII's destruction of
the English monasteries.
H, ✠

St. Ignatius Loyola (1491-1556), Spain and Italy
The Golden Thread: A Novel about St. Ignatius by Louis
de Wohl [Ignatius] – de Wohl does an amazing job
telling the story of St. Ignatius' conversion and pil-
grimage, while at the same time giving the reader a

vivid picture of sixteenth century Spain. Consider following up with de Wohl's novel *Set All Afire*.
H, A, ✠

*A Pilgrim's Journey: The Autobiography of St. Ignatius
of Loyola* edited by Joseph Tylenda, SJ [Ignatius] –
Read St. Ignatius' own words.
H, A, ✠

Saint Ignatius of Loyola by F. A. Forbes [TAN] –
Dramatic story of this great saint.
M, H, ✠

St. Ignatius and the Company of Jesus (**Vision Book**) by
August Derleth [Ignatius] – The founder of the Society
of Jesus and his story written for young teens.
M, H, ✠

St. Ignatius Loyola: For the Greater Glory of God
(**Encounter the Saints**) by Donna Giaimo, FSP and
Patricia Edward Jablonski, FSP [Pauline] – Begins
with Ignatius' childhood and his dream of becoming a
knight. However, God had other plans.
G, M, ✠

Battle of Lepanto (1571)

Lepanto by G. K. Chesterton, edited by Dale Ahlquist
[Ignatius] – Chesterton's poetry shines in this masterpiece of rhyme, rhythm, and alliteration. This Ignatius
commentary edition is worth obtaining for the
explanatory notes.
H, A, ✠

The Blood Red Crescent and the Battle of Lepanto by
Henry Garnett [Lepanto] – The author begins by let-
ting his reader know which parts of the story are history and which parts are fiction.
M, H, ✠

History

St. Edmund Campion (1540-1581), England

Edmund Campion: A Life by Evelyn Waugh [Ignatius] – The author of *Brideshead Revisited* does an outstanding job of telling St. Edmund's story.
H, A, ✠

Edmund Campion: Hero of God's Underground **(Vision Book)** by Harold Gardiner, SJ [Ignatius] – An inspiring account of St. Edmund's daring adventures. He was truly a "hero of God's underground" and was martyred for ministering to Catholics who were being persecuted at the time.
M, H, ✠

St. Philip Neri (1515-1595), Italy

St. Philip of the Joyous Heart **(Vision Book)** by Francis X. Connolly [Ignatius] – St. Philip brought converts to the church through his personal joy and love for Christ. Though wise and educated, he was simple and childlike – just as Christ calls us to be like little children.
M, H, ✠

Queen Elizabeth I (1533-1603), England

By What Authority by Robert Hugh Benson [Lepanto] – Sir Nicholas helps renegade priests hide from Queen Elizabeth's men.
H, A, ✠

Come Rack, Come Rope by Robert Hugh Benson [Neumann] – A dramatization of the suffering endured by Catholics under Elizabeth I. An undercover priest, a traitor, martyrdom, and a sweet love story. Also published by Lepanto Press.
H, A, ✠

Red Hugh, Prince of Donegal by Robert T. Reilly [Bethlehem] – Based on the true story of Hugh Roe

O'Donnel, an Irish prince at the time of Queen
Elizabeth. He fights off English invaders, endures
imprisonment, and keeps the faith. Great story for
boys.

M, H, ✠

St. Teresa of Avila (1515-1582), Spain
St. John of the Cross (1541-1591), Spain

Interior Castle by St. Teresa of Avila – Compares the soul
to a castle with many rooms. A classic work on mysti-
cal theology. This and *Dark Night of the Soul* are very
deep works.

A, ✠

Dark Night of the Soul by St. John of the Cross – A
Spanish mystic, St. John of the Cross writes about
journeying to God.

A, ✠

Fire Within: St. Teresa of Avila, St. John of the Cross,
and the Gospel by Thomas Dubay, S. M. [Ignatius] –
Read before attempting to tackle *Interior Castle* or
Dark Night of the Soul. If you like this book, check
out Father Dubay's many other excellent titles.

H, A, ✠

Saint Teresa of Avila by F. A. Forbes [TAN] – The Forbes
books are nice, easy-to-read biographies.

M, H, ✠

Mary Queen of Scots (1542-1587), Scotland

The Armada **(American Heritage Library)** by Garrett
Mattingly – The story of the Spanish Armada's defeat.
Opens with a chapter praising Queen Elizabeth, but
little bias beyond that point.

H, A

History

Gunpowder Plot (1604), England

The Gunpowder Plot by Hugh Ross Williamson
    [Neumann] – This true story is fascinating to me.
    There are still conflicting historical details to this day,
    and yet they still celebrate Guy Fawkes Day in
    England.
    H, A, ✠

St. Camillus de Lellis (1550-1614), Italy

A Soldier Surrenders by Susan Peek [Lepanto] – Once a
    soldier of fortune, with a love for alcohol and gam-
    bling, St. Camillus gave over his life to minister to the
    sick of Italy.
    H, ✠

William Shakespeare (1564-1616), England

Tales from Shakespeare by Charles and Mary Lamb –
    Several Shakespearian plays rewritten as prose. An
    excellent way to introduce children to Shakespeare
    and help them gain an overview if they aren't yet
    ready to tackle the original works.
    M, H

Shakespeare: His Work & His World by Michael Rosen,
    illustrated by Robert Ingpen – Beautiful paintings
    illustrate this book. Rosen shows the great impact
    Shakespeare has had on our culture.
    M

The Children's Shakespeare by Edith Nesbit – This
    retelling is very readable. Retains the Shakespearean
    language, but is told in an interesting prose.
    G, M

Bard of Avon: The Story of William Shakespeare by Peter
    Vennema and Diane Stanley – The life of Shakespeare
    for children.
    G, M

William Shakespeare and the Globe by Aliki – Explores the culture surrounding Shakespeare and the building of the Globe Theater.
   P, G

St. Francis de Sales (1567-1622), France
Rerum Omnium Perturbationem by Pope Pius XI (encyclical) – Written in 1923, upholding St. Francis de Sales as a model of meekness of heart and kindness.
   H, A, ✠
Saintmaker: The Remarkable Life of Francis de Sales by Michael de la Bedoyere [Sophia] – Patron saint of journalists, St. Francis was the first to make wide use of religious tracts.
   H, A, ✠

The Thirty Years' War (1618-1648), Europe
St. Vincent de Paul (1580-1660), France
St. Vincent de Paul (**Vision Book**) by Margaret Ann Hubbard – St. Vincent began as a shepherd boy, then a slave in Africa, and finally a priest to the poor. Learn how he escaped slavery to France and founded two religious orders.
   M, H, ✠
Saint Vincent de Paul by F. A. Forbes [TAN] – With the Thirty Years' War raging in the background, St. Vincent fought to care for the spiritual and physical needs of the thousands left orphaned.
   G, M, ✠

King Charles I (1600-1649), England
English Civil War (1642-1648)
The Children of the New Forest by Captain Frederick Marryat – Four orphaned children disguise themselves

as a forester's grandchildren. Their father died fighting for the Royalists in the British Civil War.
H, A, ✠

St. Margaret Mary (1647-1690), France
Saint Margaret Mary: And the Promises of the Sacred Heart of Jesus by Mary Fabyan Windeatt [TAN] – A favorite author, Windeatt tells the story of St. Margaret Mary's revelation of the Sacred Heart of Jesus. Her life wasn't easy. She had a troubled childhood, hardship in the convent, and many penances.
G, M, ✠

St. Louis Grignion of Montfort (1673-1716), France
St. Louis de Montfort: The Story of Our Lady's Slave by Mary Fabyan Windeatt [TAN] – Inspiring story of the "Apostle of Mary" who wrote *The Secret of the Rosary* and *True Devotion to Mary.*
G, M, ✠

Outlaws of Ravenhurst by Sister M. Imelda Wallace, SL [Neumann] – Set in seventeenth century Scotland, this is the story of the persecution faced by Catholics, and the faith that carried them. Also published by Lepanto Press.
M, H, ✠

Modern Europe (1700 to present)

Captain James Cook; (1728-1779), England
Magnificent Voyage: An American Adventurer on Captain James Cook's Final Expedition by Laurie Lawler – Based on the journal of American John Ledyard, who traveled with Captain Cook when he

discovered the Hawaiian Islands and searched for the
Northwest Passage.
M

Jacobite Rebellion (1745), Scotland

Kidnapped by Robert Louis Stevenson – Tricked by his
    uncle, a young lowlander is put into a precarious posi-
    tion, only to escape with the help of a Jacobite.
    H

King George III (1738-1820), England

The Reb and the Redcoats (**Living History Library**) by
    Constance Savery [Bethlehem] – The Revolutionary
    War from the perspective of a British family. A fifteen-
    year-old Patriot is taken as a prisoner of war and sent
    to England.
    M, H, ✠

Can't You Make Them Behave, King George? by Jean
    Fritz – See the American Revolution through the eyes
    of the English monarch.
    G, M

St. John Vianney (Cure of Ars) (1786-1859), France

Sermons of the Cure of Ars by St. John Vianney
    [Neumann] – Read St. John Vianney's own words. He
    was known to be a great confession priest.
    H, A, ✠

The Cure of Ars: The Priest Who Outtalked the Devil
    (**Vision Book**) by Milton Lomask [Ignatius] – An
    exciting tale of the Cure's adventures. Also provides
    insight to his simple humility.
    M, H, ✠

The Cure of Ars by Mary Fabyan Windeatt [TAN] – Told
    in the first person from St. John Vianney's perspective.

Delves into the topic of priestly vocations and so would be especially good for boys.

G, M, ✠

King Louis XVI (1754-1793), France
Queen Marie Antoinette (1755-1793), France
The French Revolution (1789-1799)
***The Guillotine and the Cross* by** Warren Carroll [Christendom] – A must read for an in-depth study of the French Revolution. Gives a view not often presented in other histories, studying the violence and turmoil accompanying the French Revolution. Compare to the American Revolution.

H, A, ✠

***The Song at the Scaffold* by** Gertrude von Le Fort [Sophia] – This is considered by many to be a classic. It is an inspirational and true story of sixteen Carmelite nuns who were guillotined during the Reign of Terror. Also reprinted by Lepanto Press and Neumann Press.

H, A, ✠

***Trianon: A Novel of Royal France* by** Elena Maria Vidal [Neumann] – Historical fiction of King Louis XVI and his Queen, Marie Antoinette. Delves into their love story and their Catholic faith.

H, A, ✠

***A Tale of Two Cities* by** Charles Dickens – The story of an Englishman who gives his life during the French Revolution to save the husband of the woman he loves. A story of sacrifice in its truest form with the bloodletting of the French Revolution in the backdrop.

H, A

The Scarlet Pimpernel by Baroness Orczy Emmuska –
The Scarlet Pimpernel is the original "masked
avenger."
H

St. Julie Billiart (1751-1816), France
Saint Julie Billiart: The Smiling Saint **(Encounter the
Saints)** by Mary Kathleen Glavich, SND [Pauline] –
St. Julie hid loyal priests in her home during the
French Revolution. She was forced to flee and go into
hiding.
G, M, ✠

Napoleon Bonaparte (1769-1821), France
The Flying Ensign: Greencoats Against Napoleon by
Showell Styles [Bethlehem] – Ensign Peter Byrd sets
out on a mission to rescue a Spanish senorita, Anita,
and her rich, noble father who is imprisoned by the
evil bandit, El Cuchillo – "The Knife."
M, H, ✠

The **Midshipman Quinn Collection** by Showell Styles
[Bethlehem] – Set in 1803 France, this book is four
separate stories of a junior British officer, fighting
Napoleon. Strategic battle plans, suspense, great
escapes, and more.
M, H, ✠

The Bourbon Restoration (1814-1830), France
Madame Royale by Elena Maria Vidal [Neumann] –
Sequel to *Trianon.* Focuses on the daughter of Louis
XVI and Marie Antoinette, and her search for her lost
brother.
H, A, ✠

The Switherby Pilgrims: A Tale of the Australian Bush
(Living History Library) by Eleanor Spence

[Bethlehem] – Miss Arabella wants to help ten orphans in her care escape 1820's England and its factory grime. She takes them to Australia, where she has a land grant.
G, M

Ven. Pauline Jaricot (1799-1862), France
Pauline Jaricot by Mary Fabyan Windeatt [TAN] – Tells of how Venerable Pauline was cured by St. Philomena, and her work in spreading the Catholic faith.
G, M, ✠

St. Catherine Laboure (1806-1876), France
St. Catherine Laboure and the Miraculous Medal (**Vision Book**) by Alma Power-Waters [Ignatius] – The Vision Book Series was originally published decades ago and was a Catholic school staple.
M, H, ✠

The Miraculous Medal by Mary Fabyan Windeatt [TAN] – Tells of St. Catherine's vision of Our Lady and her gift of the Miraculous Medal.
G, M, ✠

St. John Bosco (1815-1888), Italy
St. Dominic Savio (1842-1857), Italy
Saint John Bosco by F. A. Forbes [TAN] – The life of young Dominic, told in such a compelling way teenagers will want to imitate this holy teen.
M, H, ✠

St. John Bosco and St. Dominic Savio (**Vision Book**) by Catherine Beebe [Ignatius] – St. John Bosco, the patron saint of boys, built schools that were known to be cheerful places to learn and had high school spirit. He used juggling, magic, and acrobats to evangelize

History

boys and girls. His best-loved student also became a saint – St. Dominic.

G, M, ✠

Karl Marx (1818-1883), Germany

The Marx-Engels Reader by Karl Marx, et al – To truly understand Marxism, it's important to read Marx's own words. Make sure to thoroughly discuss with your student and follow up with *Rerum Novarum*.
 H, A

Rerum Novarum by Pope Leo XIII (encyclical) – *On the Condition of Workers*. Written in 1891, supports the right of workers to organize, but rejects socialism.
 H, A, ✠

St. Pope Pius X (1835-1914), Italy

Pope St. Pius the X by F. A. Forbes [TAN] – A great biography. Includes his challenge to his flock to "restore all things in Christ." Pope St. Pius X fought for a proper interpretation of "separation of church and state."
 M, H, ✠

St. Pius X: The Farm Boy Who Became Pope (Vision Book) by Walter Dietheim OSB [Ignatius] – Giuseppe Sarto began as a simple farm boy, went on to be a country priest, and eventually became pope. He was humble in spirit and never forgot the poor. He was known as the "Pope of Little Children."
 M, H, ✠

St. Bernadette (1844-1879), France
Our Lady of Lourdes (1858)

Bernadette: Our Lady's Little Servant (Vision Book) by Herta Pauli [Ignatius] – An engaging account of humble Bernadette who meets Our Lady of in the grotto at Lourdes.

M, H, ✠

Saint Bernadette Soubirous: Light in the Grotto **(Encounter the Saints)** by Anne Eileen Heffernan, FSP and Mary Elizabeth Tebo, FSP [Pauline] – As a child, St. Bernadette suffered from chronic asthma and terrible poverty, yet she changed the world.

G, M, ✠

Under a Changing Moon by Margot Benary-Isbert [Bethlehem] – Takes place in 1860's Germany. A 17-year-old girl comes home after two years in boarding school.

H, ✠

St. Therese of Lisieux (1873-1897), France

Story of a Soul by St. Therese [Ignatius] – A beloved saint as well as a Doctor of the Church, this is St. Therese's autobiography and the story of her "little way." A spiritual masterpiece of simplicity and virtue.

H, A, ✠

St. Therese and the Roses **(Vision Book)** by Helen Walker Homan [Ignatius] – Gives insight to the little details of St. Therese's childhood.

M, H, ✠

The Little Flower: The Story of St. Therese of the Child Jesus by Mary Fabyan Windeatt [TAN] – Sweet story of a once-spoiled little girl and how she grew into a saint.

G, M, ✠

Little Therese: The Life of St. Therese for Children by Pere J. Carbonel, S.J. [Catholic Heritage Curricula] – Emphasis on her childhood and family life. Shows

children St. Therese wasn't a perfect child, but worked
hard in her "little way" to please Jesus.

G, M, ✠

St. Therese of Lisieux: The Little Way of Love
(Encounter the Saints) by Mary Kathleen Glavich,
SND [Pauline] – A down-to-earth portrayal of a great
saint.

G, ✠

St. Padre Pio (1887-1968), Italy

Saint Pio of Pietrelcina: Rich in Love **(Encounter the
Saints)** by Eileen Dunn Bertanzetti [Pauline] – Padre
Pio suffered greatly in his life. He was graced with the
stigmata. He is said to have had many spiritual gifts
and started an Italian hospital, which today treats
60,000 patients a year.

G, M, ✠

Railway Children by E. Nesbit – Takes place in 1900's
England. This is a great story for a read aloud. Four
children must help their mother through a trying time.
Moving far out to the country, they manage to
befriend various folks at the railroad station nearby. A
wonderful reunion results at the end.

M, H

Andries by Hilda van Stockum [Bethlehem] – Another
great read aloud. This story set in the 1900's revolves
around a lonely boy who is befriended by a nearby
family. The homey atmosphere of the family brings
Andries out of his shell and the friendships forged are
priceless.

M, H, ✠

The Good Master by Kate Seredy – A great insight to the
Catholic culture of pre-WWI Hungary. This beautiful

story is about a spoiled city girl and her transformation
after being sent to the country to stay with family.
M

World War I (1914-1917)

***Testament of Youth: An Autobiographical Study of the
Years 1900-1925*** by Vera Britten – The autobiography
of a young woman who spent the war as a nurse in
England and France. Her beloved brother, her fiancée,
and their two best friends were all killed. Brings home
the realities of WWI.
H, A

The Singing Tree by Kate Seredy – Sequel to *The Good
Master*. Set in WWI Hungary, tells how a family survives. Younger students will enjoy the story, while
older students can appreciate the depth of the political
undertones.
M

Charlotte Sometimes by Penelope Farmer – Time slip
allows a schoolgirl to move between the 1960's and
WWI.
G, M

War Game by Michael Foreman – Four young men from
England go to fight in the trenches. Tells the story of
the famous football match in No Man's Land on
Christmas Day 1914.
G

War Horse by Michael Morpurgo – Story of a farm horse
sold to the army and sent to the Western Front in
1914.
G

Fatima (1917), Portugal

1917: Red Banners, White Mantle by Warren Carroll
[Christendom] – Relates the events of 1917, month by

month. World War I, Emperor Charles of Austria, the rise of Lenin, and the apparitions of Our Lady in Portugal.

H, A, ✠

***Our Lady Came to Fatima* (Vision Book)** by Ruth Fox Hume [Ignatius] – Learn not only about the apparition of the Blessed Mother, but about Lucia, Jacinta, and Francisco's parents, neighbors, and village.

M, H, ✠

The Children of Fatima by Mary Fabyan Windeatt [TAN] – A lovely story of the three shepherd children of Fatima and their adventures.

G, M, ✠

***Blessed Jacinta and Francisco Marto: Shepherds of Fatima* (Encounter the Saints)** by Anne Eileen Heffernan , FSP and Patricia Edward Jablonsky, FSP [Pauline] – Learn about the three visionaries and how they brought the Blessed Mother's message to the whole world.

G, M, ✠

Mahatma Gandhi (1869-1948), India

Gandhi by Demi – Beautifully illustrated biography.

G

Russian Revolution (1917)
Vladimir Lenin (1870-1924), Russia

Angel on the Square by Gloria Whelan – Prequel to *The Impossible Journey*, gives a peek inside the Romanov household and the Russian Revolution.

M

Joseph Stalin (1879-1953), Russia

The Impossible Journey by Gloria Whelan – My children and I listened to this book on tape while vacationing.

It is the moving story of two children searching for
their parents who were sent to Siberia by Stalin's
henchmen.
M

***The Drovers Road Collection: Adventures in New
Zealand*** by Joyce West [Bethlehem] – This set of
three books in one (*Drovers Road*, *Cape Lost*, and *The
Golden Country*) takes place in 1920s–1930s New
Zealand.
M, H, ✠

Bantry Bay Series by Hilda van Stockum [Bethlehem] –
We loved reading these 1930s Irish tales out loud. Van
Stockum has a way of writing in which the reader can
assume an Irish accent. The stories are each special,
revolving around incidents which take place in the
family. Touching and homey.
Cottage at Bantry Bay
Francie on the Run
Pegeen
M, H, ✠

St. Edith Stein (1891-1942), Germany

***Edith Stein: A Biography: The Untold Story of the
Philosopher and Mystic Who Lost Her Life in the
Death Camps of Auschwitz*** by Waltrand Herbstrith
[Ignatius] – The long title says it all.
H, A, ✠

Saint Edith Stein: Blessed by the Cross **(Encounter the
Saints)** by Mary Lea Hill, FSP [Pauline] – Edith Stein,
a nun, was a convert from Judaism.
G, M, ✠

St. Maximilian Mary Kolbe (1894-1941), Poland

Kolbe: Saint of the Immaculata edited by Brother Francis
    Mary, FFI [Ignatius] – Great book on St. Maximilian
    and his Immaculata Movement devoted to Our Lady.
    Called by John Paul II, "The Saint of our difficult cen-
    tury."
    H, A, ✠

Saint Maximilian Kolbe: Mary's Knight **(Encounter the
    Saints)** by Patricia Edward Jablonski, FSP [Pauline] –
    A prisoner in the Auschwitz concentration camp, St
    Maximilian offered his own life in place of another
    prisoner, a young husband and father, who was
    marked for death. He is a great martyr of the twentieth
    century.
    G, M, ✠

Blessed Pier Giorgio Frassati (1901-1925), Italy

Blessed Pier Giorgio Frassati: Journey to the Summit
    (Encounter the Saints) by Ana Maria Vazquez and
    Jennings Dean – Bl. Pier is known as "A Saint for the
    youth of the Third Millennium."
    G, M, ✠

Adolf Hitler (1889-1945), Germany

Mein Kempf by Adolf Hitler – Hitler's autobiography pub-
    lished in 1925, and the second volume in 1926, was
    dismissed at the time as nonsense. It's poorly written,
    yet is an important read in understanding how the
    Holocaust and World War II could happen. Make sure
    to discuss thoroughly and follow up with the encycli-
    cal, *Mit Brennender Sorge.*
    H, A, *

Mit Brennender Sorge by Pope Pius XI (encyclical) – One
    of the few encyclicals not written in Latin (1937). It is
    translated as "with deep anxiety." It was written

directly to the German bishops and was read in every German parish.

H, A, ✠

Hitler: A Study in Tyranny by Alan Bullock – This is considered by many as the authoritative biography of Hitler. A balanced and readable account.

H, A

When Hitler Stole Pink Rabbit by Judith Kerr – This autobiographical account is about a nine-year-old, Jewish girl. Along with her family, she escapes from Nazi Germany in 1933. A favorite book on this tragic era.

G, M

Anne Frank (1929-1945), Germany and Netherlands

The Diary of Anne Frank by Anne Frank – The book read by most school children. There are three versions: The original entries, the version Anne edited herself while in hiding, and the best known version edited by her father, Otto Frank. For younger students, use the Otto version. For older students there is a critical edition with all three versions plus commentary. Does include her thoughts on sexuality, so use caution.

M, H, *

The Story of Anne Frank (**DK Reader**) by Brenda Ralph Lewis – A simple version of Anne Frank's story.

G

Usborne – Anne Frank

World War II (1939-1945)

The Hiding Place by Corrie ten Boom – This autobiographical account takes place in Nazi-occupied Holland. A devout Christian, Corrie ten Boom, along with her family, hid many Jewish families in their clock shop until the family was arrested. I was deeply affected by the accounts of her and her sister Betsy's persecution in the concentration camp and their Christian response to the persecution.

H, A

The Endless Steppe: Growing Up in Siberia by Esther Houtzig – A ten-year-old girl and her family are sent to the forced-labor camps of Siberia when Russia invades Poland in 1941. Their crime? They were capitalists.

H, A

The Shadow of His Wings: The True Story of Fr. Gereon Goldmann, OFM [Ignatius] – The true story of a German seminarian drafted into the Secret Service at the onset of World War II. He managed to complete his priestly training and minister to war victims right under the noses of the Nazis. Very uplifting story of a horrible time in history.

H, A, ✠

***The Borrowed House* (Young Adult Historical Bookshelf)** by Hilda van Stockum [Bethlehem] – A thirteen-year-old girl, who is a member of the Hitler Youth, discovers everything she was taught is a lie when her family is forced to leave Germany for Amsterdam. A great story.

H, ✠

***The Winged Watchman* (Living History Library)** by Hilda van Stockum [Bethlehem] – Gives insight into how the Nazis courted the youth in occupied countries. This story revolves around a Dutch family who join the resistance. Shows the contrast between the evil of Nazism and the courage of those who fought them.

M, H, ✠

Escape from Warsaw by Ian Serraillier – Originally titled *The Silver Sword*, this is a true story of a Polish family

separated by the war and the hardships they endure to
reunite.

M, H

Number the Stars by Lois Lowry – Based on a true
account of the evacuation of the Jews from Nazi-occupied Denmark.

M

Enemy Brothers **(Living History Library)** by Constance
Savery [Bethlehem] – Two brothers are separated as
youths, with one being raised in Germany and the
other in England. They're unexpectedly reunited during World War II in England. A real page turner.
Interestingly, this book was written in 1943, before the
war's end.

G, M, ✠

The Small War of Sergeant Donkey **(Living History
Library)** by Maureen Daly [Bethlehem] – The war in
Italy and the Americans' participation as seen through
the eyes of a young boy and a special donkey.

G, M, ✠

Snow Treasure by Marie McSwigan – Norwegian children
smuggle out the town's gold on sleds to keep it out of
the hands of the Nazis.

G, M

Twenty and Ten by Claire Bishop – Takes place in Nazi-
occupied France where twenty school children con-
spire to hide ten Jewish children.

G, M

The Secret Seder by Doreen Rappaport, illustrated by
Emily Arnold McCully – The story of Paris Jews hiding from Nazis and celebrating the Passover in secret.

G

Pope Pius XII (papacy 1939-1958), Italy
Hitler, the War and the Pope by Ronald Rychlak [Our
   Sunday Visitor] – Important reading to refute modern
   charges against Pope Pius XII and the Church.
   H, A, ✠

Pope John XXIII (papacy 1958-1963)
Vatican II (1962-1965)
The Sixteen Documents of Vatican II edited and translated by Douglas Bushman [Pauline] – Best translation,
   includes brief introductory notes to each of the documents.
   H, A, ✠

The Rose Round **(Young Adult Historical Bookshelf)** by
   Meriol Trevor [Bethlehem] – The Catholic undertones
   of this book are interwoven throughout the story.
   H, ✠

The Miracle of St. Nicholas by Gloria Whelan
   [Bethlehem] – The Communists shut down the
   Russian village church of this story sixty years earlier.
   After the fall of Communism, the church is reopened,
   but it's empty. Then, on Christmas day, a miracle takes
   place.
   P, G, ✠

Mother Teresa of Calcutta (1910-1997), India
Mother Teresa: Missionary of Charity **(Heroes of the**
   Faith) by Sam Wellman – My daughters and I were
   moved by this book when we read it together.
   Learning about Mother Teresa's childhood and how
   her parents raised her, helped me as a mother.
   M, H

History

Blessed Teresa of Calcutta: Missionary of Charity **(Encounter the Saints)** by Mary Kathleen Glavich, SND [Pauline] – Begins with Mother's childhood in Albania and takes the reader through her missionary work. Glossary included.
G, M, ✠

The Young Life of Mother Teresa of Calcutta by Claire Jordan Mohan [Young Sparrow Press] – For educators, includes timeline, list for further reading, and quotes.
G, M, ✠

Mother Teresa by Demi – A beautiful picture book, detailing Mother Teresa's work with the poor and infirmed.
G

Pope John Paul II (papacy 1978-2005), Poland

Witness to Hope: The Biography of Pope John Paul II by George Weigel – With unprecedented access to Pope John Paul II, Weigel wrote a comprehensive biography. This is not a short, easy read, but is so rich in historical and personal detail it's well worth the effort.
H, A, ✠

Karol From Poland: The Life of Pope John Paul II for Children **(Encounter the Saints)** by M. Leonora Wilson, FSP [Pauline] – A nice little chapter book on the life of Pope John Paul II.
G, M, ✠

Pope John Paul II Comic Book by Toni Pagot [Pauline] – Fun and colorful way to introduce children to John Paul II.
G, M, ✠

The Young Life of Pope John Paul II by Claire Jordan Mohan [Young Sparrow Press] – Easy chapter book on John Paul II's childhood.
G, M, ✠

History

The Americas

Pre-Columbian Era – Prehistory to 1492

Age of Exploration / Colonialism – 1492 to 1776

The Earliest Americans by Helen Roney Sattler –
Chronicles the arrival of man to North America. A
study in migration, archeology, climate changes, and
so on.
M

Native American Shipwrecks by James P. Delgado –
Studying Native Americans through shipwrecks is a
neat way to learn about history.
G, M

Stories of Great Americans for Little Americans (**Lost
Classics**) by Edward Eggleston – Originally written in
1895, this is a collection of stories about American
historical figures for children.
G

The Children's Book of America edited by Bill Bennett –
Bennett takes familiar tales from American history and
folklore and puts them into bite-size pieces for grade
school children.
G

Juan Ponce de Leon (c. 1460-1521)

Ponce de Leon by Wyatt Blassingame – This picture book
looks at the political forces and personal ambition that
eventually brought Ponce de Leon to Florida.
G, M

Hernando Cortez (1485-1547)

Montezuma II (1480-1520)

The Custer Legacy by Bruce T. Clark – A history mystery,
which takes you from Montezuma in 1520 to the Old
West and finally to Vatican City in the twentieth cen-

tury. My teen son really enjoyed this book.

H, A, ✠

Our Lady of Guadalupe and the Conquest of Darkness
by Warren Carroll [Christendom] – Despite its title,
the impact of Our Lady of Guadalupe is not explored
until the end. This history chronicles the conquest of
Mexico from the world-view of the Spanish conquista-
dors.

H, A, ✠

Our Lady of Guadalupe (1531)
St. Juan Diego (1471-1548), Mexico

Not Made by Human Hands by Thomas Sennot [Ignatius]
– Presents scientific evidence for the authenticity of
St. Juan Diego's tilma as well as the Shroud of Turin.

H, A, ✠

Saint Juan Diego and Our Lady of Guadalupe
(Encounter the Saints) by Josephine Nobisso
[Pauline] – A nice little chapter book, which is an easy
read.

G, M, ✠

The Lady of Guadalupe by Tomie dePaola – Beautifully
illustrated, this children's book is also available in
Spanish.

G, ✠

Sir Walter Raleigh (c. 1554-1618)
Squanto or Tisquaantum (d. 1622)

Squanto, Friend of the Pilgrims by Clyde Robert Bulla –
Written in 1954, this is still a classroom staple.

M

Squanto's Journey: The Story of the First Thanksgiving
by Joseph Bruchac – Tells the incredible story of
Squanto and all he endured.

G

History

Captain John Smith (c. 1580-1631)
Pocahontas (c. 1595-1617)

Pocahontas by Ingri and Edgar d'Aulaire – Pocahontas
was an incredible young woman and modern tales of
her life do her a great injustice. This is a wonderfully
illustrated book, which will give children an insight to
the real Pocahontas.

G, M

Pocahontas + the Strangers

Jamestown Founded (1607)

A Lion to Guard Us by Clyde Robert Bulla – Based on an
actual incident in 1609. Three children travel alone to
the colonies in search of their father.

G, M

St. Francis Solano (1549-1610), Peru and Argentina

Saint Francis Solano by Mary Fabyan Windeatt [TAN] –
Children enjoy following the adventures of St. Francis
Solano, including how he converted 9,000 Indians
with a single sermon.

G, M, ✠

St. Rose of Lima (1586-1617), Peru

Saint Rose of Lima by Mary Fabyan Windeatt [TAN] –
Sweet story of a child who had a great love for God.

G, M, ✠

St. John Masias (1585-1635), Peru

St. John Masias by Mary Fabyan Windeatt [TAN] –
Fascinating story of St. John Masias who was known
to levitate, prophesy, and work many miracles.

G, M, ✠

History

Mayflower (1620)

Mourt's Relation: A Journal of the Pilgrims at Plymouth
edited by Dwight Heath – Details the daily life of the
Pilgrims during their first year in the Americas.
M, H

The Landing of the Pilgrims (**Landmark Book**) by James
Daughtery – Daugherty drew on the Pilgrims' own
journals to write his account of their quest for religious freedom.
G, M

On the Mayflower by Kate Waters – Make sure to check
the back of the book where the author explains her
research and distinguishes fact from her fictional story.
G

Who's That Stepping on Plymouth Rock? by Jean Fritz –
The history of the actual rock, now a monument.
G

Treasure Island by Robert Louis Stevenson – The ultimate
swashbuckling adventure. Shiver me timbers!
M, H

Flint's Island (**Adventure Library**) by Leonard Wib-
berley [Bethlehem] – Wibberley writes a sequel to
Treasure Island. Set in 1600s Caribbean.
M, H, ✠

St. Jean de Brebeuf (1593-1649)
First Jesuit to arrive in Canada (1625)
*Saints of the American Wilderness: The Brave Lives and
Holy Deaths of the Eight American Martyrs* by John
O'Brien [Sophia] – 1600s Canada was a dangerous
place for Catholic priests. Still, they came and
preached. Despite the cartoonish cover, this is a seri-

ous book with detailed descriptions of the brutalities inflicted upon the martyrs.

H, A, ✠,*

St. Martin de Porres (1579-1639), Peru

Saint Martin de Porres by Mary Fabyan Windeatt [TAN] – I love this story. St. Martin is the model of Christian humility and love. A gentle spirit, he was known to have many spiritual gifts, including bilocation.
G, M, ✠

Saint Martin de Porres: Humble Healer **(Encounter the Saints)** by Elizabeth Marie DeDomenico, FSP [Pauline] – St. Martin was born of a Spanish gentleman and a freed black woman. As a barber-surgeon, he brought his healing skills to people of all races.
G, M, ✠

Nacar, the White Deer: A Story of Mexico by Elizabeth Borton de Trevino [Bethlehem] – Takes place in 1630 with the Viceroy of Mexico anxiously awaiting a Spanish galleon bearing a special gift: a rare white deer with pink eyes and horns like pearl, thus named Nacar, Spanish for the pearly inside of a shell, *concha nacar.*
G, M

George Calvert, Lord of Baltimore (c.1580-1632)
Maryland becomes a territory (1632)

Lord Baltimore: English Politician and Colonist **(Colonial Leaders)** by Loree Laugh – Biography of the Catholic Baron who founded Maryland.
G

St. Isaac Jogues (1607-1646), France and North America

St. Isaac and the Indians **(Vision Book)** by Milton Lomask [Ignatius] – Missionary to the Iroquois, their bitter enemies the Huron and the Mohawk, St. Isaac was brutally tortured and martyred.
M, H, ✠

St. Isaac Jogues: With Burning Heart **(Encounter the Saints)** by Christine Virginia Orfeo, FSP and Mary Elizabeth Tebo, FSP [Pauline] – Tells the story of the Jesuit priest from France who came to bring the Word of God to the Native Americans.
G, M, ✠

Bl. Marie of the Incarnation (1599-1617), Canada

Blessed Marie of New France: The Story of the First Missionary Sisters in Canada by Mary Fabyan Windeatt [TAN] – Bl. Marie, a missionary sister, came to the New World in the face of many hardships to bring the Faith to the Indians.
G, M, ✠

Bl. Kateri Tekakwitha (1656-1680), United States & Canada

Kateri Tekakwitha: Mohawk Maid **(Vision Book)** by Evelyn M. Brown [Ignatius] – Though it meant being ostracized by her tribe, Bl. Kateri chose to be baptized a Catholic. Dying at the young age of twenty-four, she dedicated her life to Christ.
M, H, ✠

Kateri Tekakwitha: Mystic of the Wilderness **(Saints You Should Know)** by Margaret Bunson [Our Sunday Visitor] – Bl. Kateri is also known as the Lily of the Mohawks. This beautiful book tells her story as well as describing life for Native Americans in seventeenth century Canada.

M, H, ✠

Louis Joliet (1645-1700) and Father Jacques Marquette (1637-1675)

Fr. Marquette and the Great Rivers **(Vision Book)** by August Derleth [Ignatius] – The great river is the Mississippi, which Fr. Marquette and Louis Joliet traveled as missionaries, though it meant torture and death.

M, H, ✠

Count Louis de Buade Frontenac (1620-1698), Canada

With Pipe, Paddle and Song: A Story of the French-Canadian Voyageurs by Elizabeth Yates [Bethlehem] – Action-filled story. My children and I enjoyed this book when we studied the Voyageurs during our circle tour of Lake Superior.

H, ✠

Madeleine Takes Command **(Living History Library)** by Ethel C. Brill [Bethlehem] – True story of a fourteen-year-old girl who defends the family fort from fierce Mohawk Indians for an entire week with little help while her parents are away.

M, H, ✠

The Courage of Sarah Noble by Alice Dalgleish – Eight-year-old Sarah accompanies her father from Massachusetts to Connecticut in 1707. A true story about trust, friendship, respect, and yes, courage.

M

History

French and Indian Wars (1689-1763)

Last of the Mohicans: A Narrative of 1757 by James Fenimore Cooper – A classic. Make sure to get an unabridged version. Originally published in 1826, includes some exciting yet graphic battle scenes. H, A, *

Indian Captive: The Story of Mary Jemison by Lois Lenski – This is the real life story of a young girl who was captured in a Shawnee raid, which also left her family dead. She was later raised as a Seneca Indian. Mary is strong, despite the horrible tragedies she endures. To read her actual memoirs, search the Internet for the *Captivity Narrative* by James Seaver. M

Priest on Horseback: Father Farmer, 1720-1786 by Eva K. Betz [Neumann] – Fr. Farmer rode across Colonial America, providing Holy Mass and administering the Sacraments to those who didn't have access to a Catholic church or priest, sometimes for years. G, M, ✠

Revolutionary War Era – 1770 to 1783

Democracy in America by Alexis deTocqueville – deTocqueville was a French political scientist who traveled the United States in the mid-1800's to study democracy in action. His insights are still relevant today, even though almost 175-years old. Essential reading for every American, especially for the student of American history or political science. H, A

American Tall Tales by Adrien Stoutenburg – There are several books of this same title, so make sure to check the author. Retells several heroic tales: Paul Bunyan,

Pecos Bill, Stormalong, Mike Fink, Davy Crockett, Johnny Appleseed, John Henry, and Joe Magarac.
G, M

A Sampler View of Colonial Life: With Projects Kids Can Make by Mary Cobb – My children enjoyed the fun, hands-on projects.
G

Benjamin Franklin (1706-1790)

The Autobiography by Benjamin Franklin – Franklin was one of a kind, successful in so many different disciplines. His autobiography is a great insight to the man.
H, A

Benjamin Franklin by Ingri and Edgar d'Aulaire – You can't go wrong with any of the d'Aulaire titles.
G, M

Ben and Me by Robert Lawson – A fun story and a good read aloud. Told through the eyes of a mouse who lives in Franklin's home. The mouse not only witnesses this founding father's greatness, but helps him along.
G, M

Bl. Junipero Serra (1713-1783), Spain, Mexico, and United States
California Missions

The Man Who Founded California by M.N. Couve de Murville [Ignatius] – Bl. Junipero established missions all along the California coast and is recognized by most historians as the "Founder of California." This particular biography is spiritual as well as historical.
H, A, ✠

Never Turn Back: Father Serra's Mission by Jim Rawls – An easy chapter book on the tenacious Bl. Junipero.

History

Though facing many personal obstacles, including a lame leg, he never gave up on his mission.
G, M

Song of the Swallows by Leo Politi – A simple picture book about the swallows returning to the San Juan Mission of Capistrano each year on the feast of St. Joseph.
P, G

Amos Fortune Free Man by Elizabeth Yates – This is a true and beautiful story of a slave who earns his freedom and then works to buy the freedom of other slaves.
M, H

George Washington (1732-1799)

Rules of Civility and Decent Behavior in Company and Conversation by George Washington – This is a neat little book (thirty pages). Washington began writing his dos and don'ts at fourteen-years old. His basic rules for life, a great primary document, provide insight to Washington's character.
G, M, H, A

George Washington by Ingri and Edgar d'Aulaire – Children will love the colorful illustrations, as well as the story of Washington's childhood up through his presidency.
G, M

George Washington's Breakfast by Jean Fritz – A little boy who shares the same name and birthday as George Washington, goes on a learning adventure to discover fun facts about his namesake.
G

Boston Tea Party (1773)

***Boston Tea Party: Rebellion in the Colonies* (Adventure in Colonial America)** by James E. Knight – More than a simple act of rebellion, the Boston Tea Party was a protest against the heavy taxes imposed by Britain, and the tea monopoly of the East India Company.
  G

Revolutionary War (1775-1783)

My Brother Sam is Dead by James and Christopher Collier – The atrocities of war are clearly depicted and swearing is abundant. If you use this book, read together and discuss in depth.
  H, *

Johnny Tremain by Esther Forbes – A must-read, especially for boys.
  M

Early Thunder by Jean Fritz – A young Tory is moved to change allegiances and join the Patriots.
  M

The Fighting Ground by Avi – A thirteen-year-old boy joins the army, unbeknownst to his mother, and is taken prisoner by the Hessians. It all takes place in a twenty-four hour period. Suspenseful.
  M

Black Heroes of the American Revolution by Burke Davis – Black soldiers, sailors, spies, scouts, guides, and wagoners who participated in the struggle for American independence are profiled, along with prints and portraits from the period.
  G, M

The World Turned Upside Down: Children of 1776 by Ann Jensen – Biographical story of a family and their

part in events leading up to, and through, the
Revolutionary War.

G

An Enemy Among Them by Deborah DeFord – A Patriot
family houses a Hessian prisoner of war. Told from the
view of the teenaged daughter. There is a romantic
aspect to the story, making this a good girl book.

M, H

Paul Revere's Ride (1773)

Paul Revere and the World He Lived In by Esther Forbes
– Written in 1942, this portrait of colonial history won
the Pulitzer Prize.

H, A

Mr. Revere and I by Robert Lawson – This is a favorite
story told through the eyes of Paul Revere's horse.

G, M

And Then What Happened, Paul Revere? by Jean Fritz –
Includes many interesting details of Revere's famous
ride. Fritz has a talent of making history inviting.

G

Patrick Henry (1736-1799)

Where was Patrick Henry on the 29th of May? by Jean
Fritz – An interesting and fun biography of Patrick
Henry.

G

Declaration of Independence (1776)

The Spirits of '76: A Catholic Inquiry by Donald D'Elia –
A scholarly book best read by an advanced history student.

H, A, ✠

Will You Sign Here, John Hancock? by Jean Fritz – A humorous biography of John Hancock, includes the story of how Hancock's signature evolved over time.
G

Samuel Adams (1722-1803)
Why Don't You Get a Horse, Sam Adams? by Jean Fritz – Fritz always gives her readers a new and different way of seeing historical figures. This book presents the opportunity to talk with your child about equity in serving our country.
G

Thomas Paine (1737-1809)
Common Sense, The Rights of Man, and Other Essential Writings by Thomas Paine – "These are the times that try men's souls." So begins Paine's first Crisis paper, *Common Sense.* It sold 150,000 copies almost overnight and helped to ignite a fire under the Patriots. Make sure to discuss thoroughly with your student as Paine's religious views are skewed.
H, A

John Adams (1735-1826)
Abigail Adams (1744-1818)
The Adams-Jefferson Letters: The Complete Correspondence Between Thomas Jefferson and Abigail and John Adams edited by Lester Cappon – A great book, especially if you like to use primary documents in your history studies. Includes introduction, headnotes, and footnotes to this exchange of letters between Jefferson and the Adamses.
H, A

Remember the Ladies: A Story about Abigail Adams (Creative Minds Biography) by Jeri Ferris – Though written for children, this is a thought-provoking biography.

G

Servant to Abigail Adams: The Early American Adventures of Hannah Cooper by Kate Connell – Story of President and Mrs. John Adams's thirteen-year-old house servant. Includes correspondence between Hannah and her brother, a printer's apprentice.

G

Thomas Jefferson (1743-1826)

***The Constitutional Thought of Thomas Jefferson* (Constitutional and Democracy Series)** by David N. Mayer – An excellent study of Jefferson the man and the political thinker. In fact, the best study. Extensively references Jefferson's own words.

H, A

Bishop John Carroll (1735-1815)
Charles Carroll of Carrolton (1737-1832)

Princes of Ireland, Planters of Maryland: A Carroll Saga, 1500-1782 by Ronald Hoffman – Biography exploring the lives of three generations of Charles Carrolls, including the last surviving signer of the Declaration of Independence. A terrific history.

H

Alexander Hamilton (1757-1804)

The Federalist: A Commentary On the Constitution of the United States by Alexander Hamilton, James Madison, et al – Thomas Jefferson wrote of this book, "The best commentary on the principles of government which

186

was ever written." Should be read by every serious
student of American history.

H, A

Benedict Arnold (1741-1801)

Traitor: The Case of Benedict Arnold **(Unforgettable
Americans)** by Jean Fritz – Arnold is a very interesting character in American history. Everyone knows his
name, but few know the complexities of his character
that led to his defection. Though a simple chapter
book, it's filled with great information.

G, M

James Madison (1751-1836)

The Great Little Madison **(Unforgettable Americans)** by
Jean Fritz – An interesting chapter book on the life of
James Madison. Though small in stature and voice,
Madison was one of the great Founding Fathers and
our fourth president.

G, M

Marquis de Lafayette (1757-1834)

Why Not, Lafayette? by Jean Fritz – The story of the
young French marquis who secretly traveled to
America to join the fight for freedom. I love his story.

G

St. Elizabeth Ann Seton (1774-1821)

Mother Seton and the Sisters of Charity **(Vision Book)** by
Alma Powers-Water – After the death of her husband,
St. Elizabeth converted to Catholicism and later start-
ed the Sisters of Charity.

M, H, ✠

Kat Finds a Friend: A St. Elizabeth Ann Seton Story
(Glory of America) by Joan Stromberg [Ecce Homo]

– The Glory of America Series is a favorite of my children. Each story has a child protagonist whose life is profoundly changed by a saint. I love the illustrations of Mother Seton in this book. So often, she is depicted as a dowdy, old woman. Here we see her as a lovely, young mother.

G, M, ✠

St. Elizabeth Ann Seton: Daughter of America **(Encounter the Saints)** by Jeanne Marie Grunwell [Pauline] – Easy-to-read chapter book on the life of Mother Seton. She started the first parochial school in America and is patron to Catholic school teachers.

G, M, ✠

John Chapman (Johnny Appleseed) (1774-1845)

The Story of Johnny Appleseed by Aliki – This is a simple, little biography. A classic American tale.

P, G

The Captive by Joyce Hanson – Taking place in 1788, a son of an African chief is taken captive and eventually sold as a slave in America. Based on an actual journal.

M, H

Constitution Ratified (1789)

The Constitution of the United States – Read and study the actual document. I have my students memorize the preamble.

G, M, H, A

Shh! We're Writing the Constitution by Jean Fritz – Though an easy read, this is a detailed account of the writing of the Constitution.

G

Modern America – 1784 to Present

Sam Houston (1793-1863), Mexico and United States
Make Way for Sam Houston **(Unforgettable Americans)**
by Jean Fritz – The self-educated Houston is quite a
colorful character in American history. Though he
seems bigger than life, Fritz is able to make Houston
real for her readers.
M

Sojourner Truth (1797-1883), USA
*Walking the Road to Freedom: A Story about Sojourner
Truth* by Jeri Ferris – The Jeri Ferris books are short
easy reads, but very good. Similar in style to Jean
Fritz's books.
G

Downright Dencey **(Young Adult Historical Library)** by
Caroline Dale Snedeker [Bethlehem] – Takes place in
the early 1800's on the Island of Nantucket in a
Quaker community.
H, ✠

Lewis and Clark Expedition (1804-1806)
*The Food Journal of Lewis and Clark: Recipes for an
Expedition* by Mary Gunderson – Includes maps, historical notes, sources, and websites. Recipes are interspersed with actual entries from Lewis and Clark's
journals.
M, H

The Captain's Dog by Roland Smith – Written from the
viewpoint of Lewis' dog, Seaman. Each chapter begins
with an excerpt from Lewis' journal.
M

Of Courage Undaunted: Across the Continent with Lewis and Clark by James Daugherty – Details the incredible journey of Lewis and Clark across unmapped land.
G, M

Lewis and Clark: A Prairie Dog for the President (Step-Into-Reading, Step 3) – A captivating book for young children.
P, G

War of 1812

The Powder Monkey by George J. Galloway – A great seafaring novel set in the War of 1812. Catholic undertones throughout the story. More than one book has this title, so check author when choosing.
M, H, ✠

Once Upon This Island by Gloria Whelan – Written through the eyes of a twelve-year-old girl, left to tend the farm with her siblings, while their father is fighting in the war. Takes place on Mackinac Island in Michigan.
M, H

Tecumseh: Shawnee Leader (Let Freedom Ring Series) by Susan Gregson – Biography of the Shawnee Indian leader's fight to regain Indian territory and his part in the War of 1812.
G, M

Jean Lafitte: Pirate Hero of the War of 1812 (The Library of Pirates) by Aileen Weintraub – My young boys got a kick out of reading how a pirate helped in the War of 1812.
P, G

The Man Without a Country by Edward E. Hale – This fictional story was written in 1863 to stir up patriotism

in the North during the Civil War. A thought-provoking read.

H, A

Cleared for Action! Four Tales of the Sea by Stephen
Meader [Bethlehem] – Four nautical adventures in
one: *Clear for Action* (War of 1812); *Whaler Round
the Horn* (1830's); *Voyage of the Javelin* (1850's); and
Phantom of the Blockade (Civil War).

M, H, ✠

***They Loved to Laugh* (Young Adult Historical
Bookshelf)** by Kathryn Worth [Bethlehem] – Takes
place in 1830's North Carolina. This book is based on
a true story of the author's family. A sixteen-year-old
orphaned girl goes to live with a Quaker family. A
great story for girls, also teaches about the Quaker
way of life.

M, H, ✠

**St. John Nepomucene Neumann (1811-1860), Bohemia
and United States**

A Bishop, A Saint: The Life of St. John Neumann by Fr.
James J. Galvin [Neumann] – It's only fitting
Neumann Press would publish this title. St. John
Neumann was the first canonized saint of the United
States. There were too many priests in Bohemia, so he
was sent to America.

M, H, ✠

***Thomas Finds a Treasure: A St. John Neumann Story*
(Glory of America)** by Joan Stromberg [Ecce Homo]
– Young Thomas' father works on the Erie Canal with
many other Bohemian immigrants. Thomas finds himself victim to some local bullies, but is rescued by a
young priest, Fr. John Neumann.

G, M, ✠

Elizabeth Stanton (1815-1902)
Susan B. Anthony (1820-1906)
You Want Women to Vote, Lizzie Stanton? by Jean Fritz –
  Stanton's life story and how she became involved in
  the Suffrage movement with Susan B. Anthony.
  G

Two Years Before the Mast: A Personal Narrative by
  Richard Henry Danam Jr. – Ralph Waldo Emerson
  wrote of this narrative, "Possesses the romantic charm
  of Robinson Crusoe." It's the actual account, a trave-
  logue of sorts, of a two-year voyage by a sailor on a
  clipper ship in the 1830's.
  H, A
Amistad: A Long Road to Freedom by Walter Dean Myers
  – A factual account of the Amistad incident (1839)
  upon which the movie was based. The slave trade was
  horribly ugly, so parents may want to read this alongside their student.
  M, H, *

Stonewall Jackson (1824-1863)
Stonewall **(Unforgettable Americans)** by Jean Fritz –
  Stonewall Jackson was known to be a brilliant, yet
  eccentric, general for the Confederacy.
  G, M

Abraham Lincoln (1806-1865)
The Day Lincoln Was Shot by Jim Bishop – A minute-by-
  minute account of the day Abraham Lincoln was
  assassinated.
  H, A
Lincoln: A Photobiography by Russell Freedman – I enjoy
  Freedman's books. He chronicles his subjects' lives

through period drawings and photographs in addition to the written text.
M, H

Abraham Lincoln by Ingri and Edgar d'Aulaire – A great biography for children.
G, M

Just a Few Words, Mr. Lincoln **(All Aboard Reading, Level 3)** by Jean Fritz – All about the Gettysburg Address.
G

Abe Lincoln's Hat **(Step into Reading, Step 3)** by Martha Brenner – A simple picture book, which will introduce children to Lincoln in a fun way. Did you know Lincoln used his hat as a filing cabinet?
P, G

Blessed Francis Seelos (1819-1867)
Willie Finds Victory: A Blessed Francis Seelos Story **(Glory of America)** by Joan Stromberg [Ecce Homo] – Young Willie searches for his brother-in-law in order to take his place in the Union Army. Father Seelos steps in to help Willie.
G, M, ✠

Harriet Tubman (1820-1913)
Go Free or Die: A Story about Harriet Tubman **(Creative Minds)** by Jeri Ferris – A very readable biography of an incredible woman. After finding her way to freedom, Tubman went back, again and again, to help other slaves escape.
G

The Santa Fe Trail (1822-1880)
Tree in the Trail by Holling C. Holling – I love the Holling books. This title tells the story of a cotton-

wood tree and the history it witnesses on the Santa Fe Trail.
G, M

***Josephina's Story Collection* (American Girls)** by Valerie Tripp – I was pleasantly surprised at the respect shown to Josephina's Catholic faith in these books.
G

The Quilt-Block History of Pioneer Days by Mary Cobb – History and art projects all rolled up into one neat book.
G

Sitting Bull (c.1831-1890)
A Boy Called Slow by Joseph Bruchac – A colorful picture book about Sitting Bull as a child.
P, G

Underground Railroad (c.1835-1860)
Anthony Burns: The Defeat and Triumph of a Fugitive Slave by Virginia Hamilton – Takes place in 1854. Burns was a 20-year-old Virginia slave who escaped to Boston, putting to test the Fugitive Slave Act of 1850.
M

Brady by Jean Fritz – It's 1836 and a farm boy in Pennsylvania discovers a stop on the Underground Railroad. He finds himself caught up in the anti-slavery conflict and must choose right from wrong. Could provide a link for discussing the abortion conflict in this country today.
G, M

Sweet Clara and the Freedom Quilt by Deborah Hopkinson – This adorable story is about a slave girl who works in the big house. She takes scraps of fabric to make a quilt and sews the route of the Underground

Railroad into the pattern of the quilt to help other slaves.
G

The Oregon Trail (1841-1870)

The Oregon Trail by Francis Parkman, Jr. – A firsthand account of Parkman's 1846 trek from St. Louis, over the Oregon Trail, down the Front Range, and back again via the Santa Fe Trail.
H, A

Miles' Song by Alice McGill – A 12-year-old's transformation from complacent house slave to potential runaway in a historical novel set in a South Carolina slave plantation in 1851.
M

Brave Buffalo Fighter **(Young Adult Historical Bookshelf)** by John D. Fitzgerald [Bethlehem] – Told in diary form, details the 1860 journey of a family from St. Joseph, Missouri to Fort Laramie in Wyoming. A great story.
M, ✠

Pierre Jean de Smet (1801-1873), Belgium and U.S.

Life, Letters and Travels of Father Pierre-Jean de Smet, S.J.: 1801-1873 by Pierre-Jean de Smet [Narrative Press] – Great source material. Follow Father's mission work and learn all about Western history at the same time.
H, A, ✠

Giant of the Western Trail: The Life of Father Peter de Smet by Michael McHugh, SJ [Neumann] – Fr. de Smet was a missionary to Native Americans from 1838 to 1875. Lots of interesting details about their daily lives as well as the Church's stance on human rights.

M, ✠

Harriet Beecher Stowe (1811-1896)

Uncle Tom's Cabin by Harriet Beecher Stowe – Written with the specific purpose of protesting legalized slavery. It is a book that inflamed a nation.

H

Harriet Beecher Stowe and the Beecher Preachers **(Unforgettable Americans)** by Jean Fritz – Biography of *Uncle Tom's Cabin's* author. Tells how the book came to be written and published, as well as the public's reaction and how it changed Stowe's life.

M

The Civil War (1861-1865)

The Red Badge of Courage by Stephen Crane – A classic, this book originally appeared in serial form. Civil War veterans praised Crane for his accuracy in describing the horror of war.

H, A

Banners at Shenandoah: A Story of Sheridan's Fighting Calvary by Bruce Catton – Catton, a leading Civil War historian, tells the story of a seventeen-year-old Michigan boy who served under General Sheridan in the Union Army.

H, A

Undying Glory: The Story of the Massachusetts 54th Regiment by Clinton Cox – Account of the formation and valiant record of the first black regiment, from firing on Fort Sumter to an 1887 reunion. This story is also told in the film *Glory*.

M

The Forgotten Heroes: The Story of the Buffalo Soldiers
by Clinton Cox – Follow up to *Undying Glory*. After
the Civil War, two U.S. Cavalry regiments of African
American soldiers were assigned to the frontier to
uphold law and order, protect settlers, carry the mail,
and solve the "Indian problem."
M

Little House on the Prairie Series by Laura Ingalls
Wilder – This classic series is a must-read.
Little House in the Big Woods
Little House on the Prairie
Farmer Boy
On the Banks of Plum Creek
By the Shores of Silver Lake
The Long Winter
Little Town on the Prairie
These Happy Golden Years
The First Four Years
G, M

Secret of the Andes by Ann Nolan Clark – Takes place
four centuries after the Spanish conquest. A boy born
of royal Inca blood learns about the traditions and culture of his ancestors. He lives in the valleys of the
Andes Mountains of Peru, tending llamas.
M

Patrick Healy (c.1834-1910)
Dream of an Outcaste: Patrick F. Healy by Albert S.
Foley – Healy was a Jesuit and the first black presi-
dent of Georgetown University.
H, A, ✠

History

Booker T. Washington (1856-1915)

Up From Slavery by Booker T. Washington – This book should be read by every child studying slavery. It has been very much neglected in recent times. There is an excerpt from it in William Bennet's *Book of Virtues* if you would like a preview.

M, H, A

Fr. Damien, Martyr of Molokai (1840-1888), Kingdom of Hawaii

Father Damien and the Bells (Vision Book) by Arthur and Elizabeth Sheehan – How many Americans know the Island of Molokai in Hawaii once supported a leper colony? Fr. Damien cared for the poor outcasts, even though it meant contracting the disease himself. Inspirational.

M, H, ✠

Anne of Green Gables by L. M. Montgomery – This classic tale takes place in late 1800's Prince Edward Island, Canada. Anne is an orphaned girl filled with imagination and joy. Based on the childhood memories of the author.

M, H

Old Sam: Dakota Trotter by Don Alonzo Taylor [Bethlehem] – Two books in one that take place in 1880's Dakota Territory. Wonderful stories about a horse, Old Sam, and two boys. Based on the pioneering experiences of the author.

M, H, ✠

Sarah, Plain and Tall by Patricia MacLachlan – A widower advertises for a wife in the late 1800's. A sweet story.

G, M

Sounder by William Armstrong – Sounder is the family coon dog, scruffy and old. This is an uncomfortable story of racism in the late nineteenth century.
M, H

St. Frances Xavier Cabrini (1850-1917), Italy and United States

Quam Aerumnosa by Pope Leo XIII (encyclical) – On Italian immigration to the U.S.
H, A, ✠

Mother Cabrini: Missionary to the World **(Vision Book)** by Frances Parkinson Keyes [Ignatius] – A young girl attends a school in New Orleans started by Mother Cabrini and learns all about the foundress and her impact on American immigrants.
M, H, ✠

The Orphans Find a Home **(Glory of America)** by Joan Stromberg [Ecce Homo] – Three orphaned girls' lives are changed when they encounter Mother Cabrini. The short unit study at the end is great.
G, M, ✠

Saint Francis Xavier Cabrini: Cecchina's Dream **(Encounter the Saints)** by Victoria Dority, MSC and Mary Lou Andes, MSC [Pauline] – Written by two sisters from Mother Cabrini's order, the Missionary Sisters of the Sacred Heart.
G, M, ✠

Theodore Roosevelt (1858-1919)

Bully for You, Teddy Roosevelt **(Unforgettable Americans)** by Jean Fritz – Homeschooled children may be able to relate to Teddy's "unschooled" days.
G, M

History

Klondike Gold Rush (1897-1898), Alaska
The Call of the Wild by Jack London – Classic story of a
  kidnapped dog, Arctic wilderness, and Yukon gold.
  M

All-of-a-Kind Family by Sydney Taylor – A sweet story
  that takes place in 1912 New York City. Centers on a
  Jewish immigrant family with five daughters. A
  favorite at my house.
  G, M

World War I (1914-1917)
World War I (**First Book**) by Tom McGowen – Overview
  of the war and its implications on the world politic.
  M
World War I (DK Eyewitness) – Photo essay of World War
  I. Contains some gruesome pictures depicting war
  casualties (museum recreations).
  M, *

Jose Marti (1853-1895), Cuba
Jose Marti: Cuban Patriot and Poet (**Hispanic
  Biographies**) by David Goodnough – A straightfor-
  ward biography of the poet who inspired other Cubans
  to fight for independence from the Spanish.
  M, H
Versos Sencillos: Simple Verses (**Recovering the U.S.
  Hispanic Literary Heritage**) by Jose Marti, translated
  by Manuel A. Tellechea – Marti's poetry in this bilin-
  gual edition can be enjoyed by children.
  M, H, A

St. Katherine Drexel (1858-1955)
St. Katherine Drexel: Friend of the Oppressed (**Vision
  Book**) by Ellen Tarry – A young heiress, St. Katherine

gave away her fortune to help those far less fortunate. She founded the Sisters of the Blessed Sacrament.
M, H, ✠

Katie: The Young Life of Mother Katherine Drexel by Claire Jordan Mohan [Young Sparrow Press] – Focuses on the childhood of this modern-day saint. Insight to life in Victorian-era America. Includes the story of how she came to be beatified, photos, glossary, and timeline of her life.
G, M, ✠

Saint Katherine Drexel: The Total Gift **(Encounter the Saints)** by Susan Helen Wallace, FSP [Pauline] – The first American born saint, she ministered to Native and African Americans.
G, M, ✠

Wilbur Wright (1867-1912)
Orville Wright (1871-1948)
Miracle at Kitty Hawk: The Letters of Wilbur and Orville Wright Edited by Fred C. Kelly – Correspondence between the Wright brothers, family members, and others, chronicling the building of the first successful airplanes and historic early flights. Brings the Wright brothers alive. Evidence of the constructive beauty of wonder rooted in rationality.
H, A

The Wright Brothers: How They Invented the Airplane by Russell Freedman – As with all of Freedman's books, the photographs are central to this wonderful biography.
M, H

Modern Times: The World from the Twenties to the Nineties by Paul Johnson – *National Review*

Magazine placed this in their list of top 100 books of the twentieth century.
H, A

Ann Sullivan (1866-1936)
Helen Keller (1880-1968)

The Story of My Life by Helen Keller – Left blind and deaf by scarlet fever when she was only 19-months old, this is Keller's autobiography.
H, A

The Miracle Worker by William Gibson – Gibson's play about Keller and Sullivan first appeared on Broadway and was later made into a movie.
H, A

Franklin D. Roosevelt (1882-1945)
Eleanor Roosevelt (1884-1962)

The Roosevelt Myth by John T. Flynn – A critical look at the New Deal. Rather than glorifying Roosevelt, the author looks beyond the image and to the facts.
H, A

Eleanor Roosevelt: A Life of Discovery by Russell Freedman – I would disagree Eleanor Roosevelt was the greatest first lady or a role model for all girls, but this is still an interesting read.
M, H

Under Copp's Hill (American Girl History Mystery) by Katherine Ayres – Takes place in the tenement housing of Italian and Jewish immigrants in 1908 Boston. An eleven-year-old girl joins a library club and when things begin to disappear, she falls under suspicion.
G, M

Blessed Miguel Pro (1891-1927), Mexico

Iniquis Afflictisque by Pope Pius XI (encyclical) – *On the Persecution of the Church in Mexico*. Written in 1926.
H, A, ✠

Blessed Miguel Pro: 20th Century Martyr by Ann Ball [TAN] – Ann Ball is an expert on Bl. Miguel. A short, yet well-rounded biography. Includes photographs.
H, A, ✠

Jose Finds the King: A Miguel Pro Story by Ann Ball [Ecce Homo] – Beautiful story of Bl. Miguel told through the eyes of a child. I suggest enjoying this as a read aloud, especially since it does touch on his martyrdom.
G, M, ✠

Mexican Martyrdom by Fr. Wilfrid Parsons, SJ – The true stories of the persecuted in Mexico. Few Americans realize the extent of the anti-Catholic policies of President Plutarcho Elias Calles. Many executions were carried out in the 1920's, solely based on the practice of religion.
H, A, ✠

The Great Depression (1929-1934)

The Grapes of Wrath by John Steinbeck – A Pulitzer Prize winning novel, which follows the migration of the Joad family from Oklahoma to California.
H, A, *

To Kill A Mockingbird by Lee Harper – This novel about racial injustice during the Great Depression is another Pulitzer Prize winner. It's told through the eyes of a child and yet deals with very serious issues, including rape.
H, A, *

The Seventeenth Child by Dorothy Marie Rice and Lucille Mabel Walthall Payne – The story of a seventeenth

child of black sharecroppers as told to her daughter. It's like an oral history of the Great Depression.
M, H

Bud, Not Buddy by Christopher Paul Curtis – A ten-year-old orphan runs away from his abusive foster home in 1930's Michigan, with the crazy idea that jazz musician Herman Calloway is his father.
M, *

Potato: A Tale from the Great Depression by Kate Lied – Written by an eight-year-old girl for a writing contest. The story of a family who picks potatoes to survive the Great Depression, based on the author's grandparents.
P, G

Rent Party Jazz by William Miller – The community comes up with a brilliant idea to help their neighbor who can't pay the rent.
P, G

Roll of Thunder, Hear My Cry by Mildred Taylor – An African American family faces racism head-on in 1930's Mississippi.
M, H

Let the Circle Be Unbroken by Mildren Taylor – Sequel to *Roll of Thunder.*
M, H

The Road to Memphis by Mildred D. Taylor – Third in the series.
M, H

My Heart Lies South by Elizabeth Borton de Trevino [Bethlehem] – I enjoyed this autobiography immensely. The American author marries a Mexican gentleman and her life is transformed. A lovely romance story, which also teaches about the Mexican culture of the 1930's.
H, A, ✠

World War II (1939-1945)

The Mitchells Series by Hilda van Stockum [Bethlehem]
– This series tells about a family during World War II
back in the United States and Canada.
Canadian Summer
Friendly Gables
The Mitchells: Five for Victory
M, H, ✠

The Cay by Theodore Taylor – Takes place in 1942
Caribbean. The story of a boy whose ship is torpedoed
in 1942. He finds himself on an island with an older,
black ship hand. We enjoyed the audio book read by
LeVar Burton.
M, H

Leon's Story by Leon Walter Tillage – Autobiography of
an African American sharecropper's son in 1940's
North Carolina.
M

Korean War (1950-1953), Korea and United States
Korean War **(First Book)** by Tom McGowen – An
overview of the Korean War, which includes maps and
photographs.
G, M

Fidel Castro (1926-), Cuba
Cuba for Kids **(Cuba Foundation for Kids)** by Ismael
Roque – The history of Cuba written for children,
from Columbus to Castro.
G, M

Bishop Fulton Sheen (1895-1969)
Treasure in Clay: The Autobiography of Fulton J. Sheen
[Ignatius] – Bishop Sheen was popular on television

and radio, loved by audiences all across religious boundaries. This autobiography was finished shortly before his death. He managed to live in the world, but was not of it.

H, A, ✠

The Lilies of the Field by William Barrett – Takes place in the 1960's and is the book that inspired the movie.

H, A

The Watsons Go to Birmingham – 1963: A Novel by Christopher Paul Curtis – Blends the fictional account of an African American family with the factual events of the violent summer of 1963. Parents should read it first as there is some undesirable language.

M, *

Martin Luther King, Jr. (1929-1968)

Strength to Love by Martin Luther King, Jr. – A collection of King's sermons.

H, A

Sister Anne's Hands by Marybeth Lorbiecki – A beautiful picture book about a black nun who goes to teach in a white Catholic school in the early 1960's.

G, ✠

Vietnam War (1955-1975)

When Hell Was In Session by Jeremiah Denton – Autobiography of a POW of the Vietnam War. I found it to be a moving account filled with honor, courage, and faith. However, Denton details his torture, which can be quite disturbing.

A, *

The Grunt Padre by Fr. Daniel L. Mode [CMJ Marian] –
A moving biography of Fr. Vincent Capodanno, a
Marine chaplain in the Vietnam War. He died in action
in 1967 and was the recipient of the Congressional
Medal of Honor, the Bronze Star, and three Purple
Hearts.
M, H, A, ✠

Roe vs. Wade (1973)

Evangelium Vitae by Pope John Paul II (encyclical)
The Gospel of Life. Written in 1995.
H, A, ✠

Humanae Vitae by Pope Paul VI (encyclical) – *On the
Regulation of Birth*. Written in 1968.
H, A, ✠

That's Me in Here [Pauline] – A sweet story told by a preborn baby from the moment of his creation to his
birth.
P, G, ✠

Angel In the Waters by Regina Doman [Sophia] – A lovely story of a preborn baby who talks with her guardian
angel. Also available in Spanish.
P, G, ✠

Lyndon B. Johnson (1908-1973)

The Path to Power **(The Years of Lyndon Johnson, Vol.
1)** by Robert Caro – I found Caro's biography of
Johnson's early years to be nothing short of outstanding. If you or your student enjoy this volume, make
sure to follow up with the next two in the series. The
fourth and final book is not yet finished.
H, A

History

Robert Moses (1888-1981)
The Power Broker: Robert Moses and the Fall of New York by Robert Caro – This is a masterpiece. Tells the story of the power wielded by a single man in the building and corrupting of New York City.
H, A

Dorothy Day (1897-1980)
The Long Loneliness: The Autobiography of Dorothy Day by Dorothy Day – Day details her spiritual journey, from her socialist Bohemian days to her conversion to her activism on behalf of the poor.
A, *

Ronald Wilson Reagan (1911-2004)
An American Life by Ronald Reagan – 1990 autobiography, from his birth to the end of his presidency. His other autobiography, *Where's the Rest of Me*, covers only his earlier life.
H, A

That Printer of Udell's by Harold Bell Wright – Ronald Reagan's favorite childhood book, which had a profound affect on him spiritually.
G, M, H

Science

Science can be interesting, and it can be fun. I don't know any child who doesn't love to perform science experiments at the kitchen table. The best part is children seem to learn the most when the experiment fails, and they have to figure out what went wrong.

Scientific concepts can also be learned through literature. Interesting biographies of famous, and not-so-famous, scientists can bring the scientific world alive for a child. Combined with observation skills, a well-written science book can teach a child a great deal of information, sometimes without the child even realizing it. I have found this to be true in my homeschool.

Though I do not teach science from a textbook or through a formal program until sixth grade, my children are knowledgeable in science and always score high on their standardized tests. I believe the reason for this success is a combination of giving my children science literature and my own outward enthusiasm for the subject.

My husband has been involved in educational reform for more than two decades. He often says the best educators are those who are excited about their subject matter. Not the ones with advanced degrees, but the ones who are excited. If you want to be an effective teacher, get excited about enriching your own education. I suggest reading some of the following books for your own personal enjoyment.

God is the author of science. We should keep this in mind when approaching our science studies (and all studies for that matter). If our children love God and His church, they can't help but fall in love with the world He created. Share your love of God and your love for science with your children, and you will be successful in your homeschool.

Overview

Chesterton, A Seer of Science by Stanley Jaki – In the early 1980's Dr. Jaki, respected scholar and Catholic priest, delivered a series of lectures at Notre Dame, which shocked many members of the scientific and intellectual community. Dr. Jaki claimed G. K. Chesterton had a penetrating and prophetic vision of what science is truly about, and what it's not and cannot be.

A, ✠

Miracles and Physics by Stanley Jaki [Christendom] – As both a theologian and physicist, Dr. Jaki gives us a scholarly work, which explores the loopholes in science that leave room for miracles. If this book sparks an interest, make sure to seek out Dr. Jaki's many other titles.

A, ✠

Cartoon Guide Series by Larry Gonick – Grabs the attention of teens with humor and teaches science at the same time.

Cartoon Guide to Genetics
Cartoon Guide to Physics
Cartoon Guide to the Environment

H, A, *

Five Equations That Changed the World: The Power and Poetry of Mathematics by Michael Guillen – Could be used in math or science. A Harvard instructor, the author takes you through five significant equations in physics. Told in story form.

H, A

Galileo's Commandment: An Anthology of Great Science Writing by Edmund Blair Bolles, editor – Many essays written by different scientists, beginning with Herodotus (484-425 BC). A fascinating collection.

H, A

Science

On the Shoulders of Giants: The Great Works of Physics and Astronomy edited by Stephen Hawking – The scientific writings of Copernicus, Kepler, Galileo, Newton, and Einstein, collected into one book. For the advanced student.
H, A

Wooden Book Series – Written by a variety of authors, these little books are fun, packed full of information, and inexpensive. Great for teenagers.

Essential Elements: Atoms, Quarks, and the Periodic Table by Matt Tweed – A primer on the elements. Talks about the Big Bang theory, so make sure to use this opportunity to talk about Who created the Big Bang.

A Little Book of Coincidences by John Martineau – MacBeth Derham recommends this book as, "The solar system is God's Spirograph, and this secular little book demonstrates the mathematical beauty of a created universe without trying; there are no coincidences."

Sun, Moon, and Earth by Robin Heath – All organisms respond to four major cycles: the solar and lunar day, the synodic month, and the year.
H, A

1000 Years of Catholic Scientists by Jane Meyerhofer [Ye Hedge School] – A list of nearly 200 eminent Catholic scientists since the tenth century with short biographies.
M, H, ✠

The Mystery of the Periodic Table (**Living History Library**) by Benjamin D. Wiker [Bethlehem] – Learn how the Periodic Table we know today came to be. Includes an actual Periodic Table to accompany the story. Enjoyable read.
M, H

Science

Secrets of the Universe Series by Paul Fleisher – Secrets of the Universe starts with natural law. Provides scientific principles and how they progressed. How often do you encounter an exposition of Archimedes leading to a detailed analysis of quantum mechanics in a manner accessible to the average middle school student? These books have been, for me, a singular blessing.
Liquid and Gases: Principles of Fluid Mechanics
Matter and Energy: Principles of Matter and Thermodynamics
Relativity and Quantum Mechanics: Principles of Modern Physics
Waves: Principles of Light, Electricity, and Magnetism
M, H

The New Way Things Work by David Macaulay – Through great illustrations and concise writing, the reader learns how things work from can openers to zippers to computers and more.
G, M, H

Find the Constellations by H. A. Rey – A fun introduction to astronomy.
. G, M

Magic School Bus Chapter Book Series – Based on the original picture books.
Dinosaur Detectives
Expedition Down Under
The Great Shark Escape
Penguin Puzzle
The Giant Germ
The Search for the Missing Bones
and more
G, M

Behold and See 3 by Suchi Myjak [Catholic Heritage Curricula] – Beginning science text, which reads like a living book. Contains a chapter explaining what science is and the remaining chapters on topics from physical, earth and space, and life science. Includes experiments and review questions.

G, ✠

Catholic Stories from Science 2 by Nancy Nicholson [Catholic Heritage Curricula] – Thirty-six short stories presenting scientific topics as they relate to our relationship with God. Topics are wide-ranging including physics, geology, botany, and more. Nice read-aloud.

G, ✠

Greg's Microscope by Millicent E. Selsam – If you own a microscope, this is a must read. Selsam's other science titles for children are very nice, but sadly most are out of print.

P. G

Magic School Bus Series – A fun series, which covers a wide variety of subjects. My children also love the videos.

The Magic School Bus Lost in the Solar System
The Magic School Bus Inside the Human Body
The Magic School Bus Plants Seeds
The Magic School Bus Inside the Earth
The Magic School Bus Explores the Senses
The Magic School Bus On the Ocean Floor
The Magic School Bus At the Waterworks
    and more

P, G

What's Smaller than a Pygmy Shrew? by Robert E. Wells – This book could also tie into math. Introduces molecules, atoms, and the like, to small children.

P, G

Titles by Franklyn M. Branley – An astronomer, most of his books deal with physical/earth and space science.
Flash, Crash, Rumble, and Roll
The Moon Seems to Change
The Planets in Our Solar System
Sunshine Makes the Seasons
   and more
P, G

Geology

How to Dig a Hole to the Other Side of the World by Faith McNulty, illustrated by Marc Simont – Takes you on a trip to the center of the earth and back. Educational as well as fun.
G

Rocks in His Head by Carol Otis Hurst – True story of a family man who has an obsession with collecting rocks and makes it his life's work.
P, G

Everybody Needs a Rock by Byrd Baylor – A rock hound lays out the rules for rock hunting.
P, G

Nature Study

Keeping a Nature Journal: Discover a Whole New Way of Seeing the World Around You by Clare Walker Leslie and Charles E. Roth – Filled with ideas and advice from both amateur and professional nature journalists, with an abundance of examples taken directly from a variety of journals.
A

Wild Days: Creating Discovery Journals by Karen Skidmore Rackliffe – A short easy read. Written with the homeschooling mom in mind. Includes examples from the journals of the author's children, giving chil-

Science

dren a realistic view to what their journals may look like.

A

Pocketful of Pinecones: Nature Study with the Gentle Art of Learning by Karen Andreola –Presents journaling in a way that is very natural for families to learn. The approach is thoughtful, yet informal. The suggested reading list proved most helpful.

A

The Country Diary of an Edwardian Lady by Edith Holden – A beloved classic, Holden's journal from 1906. Beautiful.

M, H, A

Audubon Society's Master Guide to Birding – The bible of field guides.

M, H, A

Titles by Jean-Henri Fabre – Illustrated with detailed drawings and paintings. An entomologist, many of Fabre's books are based on his backyard observations. Encourage your children to explore their own backyard. Highly recommended.

Fabre's Book of Insects
Social Life in the Insect World
The Life of the Spider
   and more

M. H

Peterson Field Guide Coloring Books – A multi-sensory activity in teaching children about the study of nature.

P, G

Watching Water Birds by Jim Arnosky – This beautifully illustrated book is a favorite, which introduces the reader to a variety of water birds, from loons to herons.

P, G

Way Out in the Desert by T.J. Marsh and Jennifer Ward, illustrated by Kenneth J. Spengler – Written in rhyme with illustrations that are bold and splendid, each page mentions a desert animal and her babies, with a glossary of desert terms at the end.
P, G

Titles by Thornton Burgess are enjoyable for grade school children and will spark an interest in nature science.
The Adventures of Jimmy Skunk
The Adventures of Danny Meadow Mouse
Blacky the Crow
The Adventures of Peter Cottontail
and more.
G, M

Beatrix Potter's books are a must for any home. Wonderful read alouds for preschoolers on up. Potter was more than a children's writer, she was a scientist and a botanist.
A Tale of Peter Rabbit
The Tale of Two Bad Mice
The Tale Squirrel Nutkin
The Tale of Jemima Puddle-Duck
and more.
P, G

Historical Timeline
Science of the Past Series
Science in Ancient Mesopotamia by Carol Moss
Science in Ancient Egypt by Geraldine Woods
Science in Ancient Rome by Jacqueline Harris
Science in Ancient China by George Beshore
Science in Ancient India by Melissa Stewart

Science of the Early American Indians by Beulah and Harold Tannenbaum
G, M

Archimedes (272-212 BC), Greece – Inventor and Mathematician

The Works of Archimedes – All the known works of Archimedes himself.
H, A

The Sand Reckoner by Gillian Bradshaw – This historical fiction based on the life of Archimedes could also be tied into math.
M, H

Archimedes and the Door of Science by Jeanne Bendick [Bethlehem] – A real gem, the story and illustrations present scientific principles and the details of Archimedes life clearly and enjoyably.
G, M, ✠

Galen (129-c.200), Greece – Physician, Writer, and Philosopher

Galen and the Gateway to Medicine by Jeanne Bendick [Bethlehem] – Galen was the chief physician to the gladiators. He was also the first to show arteries carry blood, not air.
G, M, ✠

Nicolaus Copernicus (1473-1543), Poland – Astronomer

On the Revolutions of Heavenly Spheres by Copernicus – This remarkable work stands as one of the supreme monuments of science. It profoundly influenced, among others, Galileo and Sir Isaac Newton.
H, A

Nicolaus Copernicus: The Earth Is a Planet by Dennis B. Fradin – Attractive picture book, which briefly introduces the reader to Copernicus's life, from childhood through his work as an astronomer.
G

Science

Andreas Vesalius (1514-1564), Belgium – Physician
On the Structure of the Human Body by Andreas Vesalius
– Originally published in 1543, features captivating
illustrations of human skeletons and musculature, plus
descriptions of the human anatomy based in part on
the author's own dissections.
H, A

Galileo Galilei (1564-1642), Italy – Mathematician,
Astronomer, and Physicist
*Galileo's Daughter: A Historical Memoir of Science,
Faith, and Love* by Dava Sobel – See Galileo through
the beautiful letters of his daughter. The author weaves
her commentary throughout.
H, A

*Copernicus, Galileo, and the Catholic Sponsorship of
Science* by Jane Meyerhofer [Ye Hedge School] – A
very fair treatment of Galileo, which is hard to find.
H, A, ✠

Sir Isaac Newton (1642-1727), England – Physicist and
Mathematician
Newton and Gravity **(Big Idea Series)** by Paul Strathern –
The books in this series are very short, easy reads, but
written for adults.
H, A

Isaac Newton: Organizing the Universe by William
Boerst – Portrays Newton's difficult childhood, in
addition to his great achievements in adulthood.
M, H

Isaac Newton and Gravity **(Science Discoveries Series)**
by Steve Parker – Describes the laws of motion in
addition to Newton's biography. Glossary included.
G, M

John Harrison (1693-1776), England – Horologist
*Longitude: The True Story of a Lone Genius Who Solved
the Greatest Scientific Problem of His Time* by Dava

Sobel – The enjoyable story of how a self-educated watchmaker solved the navigational problem that even Newton and Galileo failed to figure out.

H, A

The Man Who Made Time Travel by Kathryn Lasky, illustrated by Kevin Hawkes – Lovely picture book about Harrison's quest to measure longitude. Great example to children: we're all capable of great things.

G

Benjamin Franklin (1706-1790), U.S. – Statesman, Scientist, Inventor, and Publisher

The Benjamin Franklin Book of Easy and Incredible Experiments by Lisa Jo Rudy – Clear and simple directions for activities and experiments related to some of Franklin's major interests: weather, electricity, music, paper and printing, light, and sound.

M, H

What's the Big Idea, Ben Franklin by Jean Fritz – A fun biography, which includes some of Franklin's experiments.

G, M

Nathaniel Bowditch (1773-1838), U.S. – Mathematician and Astronomer

Carry On Mr. Bowditch by Jean Lee Latham – This is the adventure story of a poor boy who had the persistence to master navigation and eventually authored *The American Practical Navigator*, known as "the sailor's bible."

H, A

Charles Darwin (1809-1882), England Naturalist

Humani Generis **(encyclical)** by Pope Pius XII – Written in 1950, explains the Church's position on evolution.

H, A, ✠

Darwin's Black Box: The Biochemical Challenge to Evolution by Michael Behe – Explores the theory of evolution and the origin of life. The author, a bio-chemist, provides a scientific argument for the existence of God.

H, A

The Everlasting Man by G. K. Chesterton – Chesterton's treatise in answer to modern thought, including Darwin. For the advanced student.

H, A, ✠

Finding Darwin's God: A Scientists Search for Common Ground Between God and Evolution by Kenneth R. Miller – The author, a biology professor, looks for a middle ground between evolutionists and creationists. An even-handed account for the most part, but Miller does take the opportunity to slight creationists and Intelligent Design advocates.

H, A

In the Beginning . . . A Catholic Understanding of the Story of Creation and the Fall by Joseph Cardinal Ratzinger [Wm. B. Eerdmans] – From a series of homilies given by the future Pope Benedict XVI. Excellent clarification of the Church's teaching in light of modern science.

H, A, ✠

Creator and Creation by Mary Daly [Ye Hedge School] – An explanation of the Catholic perspective on the debate about origins.

M, H, ✠

Maria Mitchell (1818-1889), U.S. – Astronomer

Maria Mitchell: The Soul of an Astronomer by Beatrice Gormley – Mitchell had a comet named after her. This biography includes many photos. Note: Includes Mitchell's struggle with Christianity.

M, H

Louis Pasteur (1822-1895), France – Chemist and Microbiologist

Joseph Lister (1827-1912), Britain – Surgeon and
Medical Scientist

*Germ Theory and Its Applications to Medicine & on the
Antiseptic Principle of the Practice of Surgery*
(Great Minds Series) by Louis Pasteur and Joseph
Lister – Primary documents are great for the upper
grades. Read Pasteur and Lister's work firsthand.
H, A

Louis Pasteur: Young Scientist **(Easy Biography Series)**
by Francene Sabin – Inspirational and interesting reading of Pasteur's childhood.
G

Pasteur's Fight Against Microbes **(Science Stories
Series)** by Beverly Birch and Christian Birmingham
Loved the story about how Pasteur saved France's
wine industry.
G

Elizabeth Blackwell (1821-1910) Britain and U.S. –
Physician

Elizabeth Blackwell: The First Woman Doctor **(Easy
Biographies Series)** by Louis Sabin – Traces the early
life of Blackwell and the struggles women had to face
in studying and practicing medicine.
G

**Gregor Mendel (1822-1884), Germany and Czech
Republic** – Geneticist

Gregor Mendel: And the Roots of Genetics **(Oxford
Portraits of Science Series)** by Edward Edelson –
Mendel was abbot of the Augustinian monastery in
Brno. His discoveries later became the cornerstone of
heredity science. Though this book is about a Catholic
priest, it's clearly a secular book. Also, as a book
about genetics, there are references to human repro-

duction. Provides the opportunity to discuss Darwinism.

H, *

Wilson Bentley (1865-1931), U.S. – Naturalist

Snowflake Bentley by Jacqueline Briggs Martin, illustrated by Mary Azarian – Wilson Bentley's life's work was the study of snowflakes.

P, G

George Washington Carver (c.1861-1943), U. S. – Agricultural Chemist

George Washington Carver: His Life & Faith in His Own Words by William J. Federer – Learn about Carver's fascinating life through his personal letters.

H, A

George Washington Carver: Inventor and Naturalist **(Heroes of the Faith)** by Sam Wellman – This is from a Protestant worldview.

M

The Story of George Washington Carver **(Scholastic Biography)** by Eva Moore – A short, easy chapter book.

G

A Weed Is a Flower: The Life of George Washington Carver by Aliki – Not only educational, also morally uplifting.

P, G

Madame Marie Curie (1867-1934), France – Physical Chemist

Madame Curie by Eve Curie – This epic was written by Madame Curie's daughter in 1937. Inspirational.

H, A, *

Radioactive Substances **(Great Minds Series)** Marie Curie – Firsthand account of the painstaking research that led to Curie's discovery of radium and other

radioactive substances.
H, A

***Marie Curie's Search for Radium* (Science Stories
Series)** by Beverly Birch and Christian Birmingham –
An enjoyable and easy-to-read series for children.
G, M

Thomas Edison (1847-1931), U.S. – Inventor

***The Thomas Edison Book of Easy and Incredible
Experiments*** by James Cook – To inspire future
Edisons.
M, H

***Thomas Alva Edison: Young Inventor* (Easy Biography
Series)** by Louis Sabin – Focuses on Edison's early
years.
G

**Guglielmo Marchese Marconi (1874-1937), Italy and
England** – Physicist and Inventor

***Marconi's Battle for Radio* (Science Stories Series)** by
Beverly Birch and Christian Birmingham – History
behind the discovery of radio waves and the eventual
developments of the radio, television, and laser communication.
G, M

Robert Falcon Scott (1868-1912), Britain – Explorer

***The Worst Journey in the World: A Tale of Loss and
Courage in the Antarctic*** by Apsley Cherry-Garrand –
The author was the only surviving member of Scott's
final exploration of the South Pole. An incredible
story.
H, A

Albert Einstein (1879-1955), Germany and U.S. –
Scientist

***The Elegant Universe: Superstrings, Hidden Dimensions,
and the Quest for the Ultimate Theory*** by Brian
Greene – A good readable primer on the sometimes

complex theory of relativity.

H, A

***Einstein and Relativity* (Big Idea Series)** by Paul Strathern – Centers on the man more than his science, recounting events that shaped Einstein's personal and intellectual growth.

H, A

Dr. Jerome Lejeune (1926-1994), France – Geneticist

Life is a Blessing by Clara Lejeune [Ignatius] – This memoir, written by Dr. Lejeune's daughter, will move you to tears. Dr. Lejeune was a personal friend of Pope John Paul II. He is famous for discovering Trisomy 21, also known as Down's Syndrome. He was shunned by many in the scientific community because he stood up for the unborn and the disabled.

H, A, ✠

Francis Crick (1916-), Britain – Biophysicist

James Watson (1928-), U.S. – Geneticist and Biophysicist

***Crick, Watson, and DNA* (Big Idea Series)** by Paul Strathern – Strathern describes Crick and Watson as "a pair of comedians." Learn about genetics and DNA.

H, A, *

Stephen Hawking (1942-), England – Physicist

The Universe in a Nutshell by Stephen Hawking – Hawking is arguably the most famous scientist of our time. He fills this text with illustrations to help us through the most difficult concepts.

H, A

Hawking and Black Holes (Big Idea Series) by Paul Strathern - Makes the very complicated easy to understand. Be on guard for political correctness.

H, A

Books about Books

I am an admitted bibliophile and, just as I love to read books, I love to read books about books. The longer I homeschool, the pickier I become about the quality of books that grace my bookshelves. In talking with my fellow homeschoolers and in reading about books, I've learned to distinguish twaddle from true living literature.

Whether visiting the bookstore, library, or homeschool conference, it's a good idea to take along a good reading list. You could take this book, but keep in mind it's not exhaustive.

Since my goal in *For the Love of Literature* is to simply provide a list of books that teach core school subjects, you will not find much here in the way of fantasy, science fiction, or pieces of literature written solely for enjoyment. Missing are such books as the Chronicles of Narnia and Lord of the Rings; yet, they also have a very important place in your homeschool. They teach moral lessons and, as I illustrated in the Introduction, they provide examples of great writing. And, gosh, they're just fun to read.

Each of the following books about books, listed alphabetically, include great reading lists and would be helpful in searching out quality books for yourself and your children. Remember to check your library before purchasing.

Books Children Love: A Guide to the Best Children's Literature (Revised Edition) by Elizabeth Wilson
Written by a homeschooling mother who uses the Charlotte Mason approach to education. A popular book, the reading list is extensive and separated by topic. Note: Several suggested titles are out of print and/or from a Protestant worldview. Check for avail-

ability and content before using her suggestions.

A

Books that Build Character: A Guide to Teaching Your Child Moral Values through Stories by William Kilpatrick and Gregory & Suzanne Wolfe - The extensive book list gives summaries on each of the recommended books. Very good.

A

Catholic Mosaic by Cay Gibson [Hillside] – Picture books ordered by the liturgical year. Mini-unit studies included for several of the books. Discussion questions, vocabulary words, copy work, activities, and observations are included in the units. Great for parents or teachers of preschool and grade school children.

A, ✠

Designing Your Own Classical Curriculum: A Guide to Catholic Home Education by Laura Berquist [Ignatius] – One of my favorite homeschooling books, it's worth the price just for the literary suggestions.

A, ✠

Kolbe Academy Recommended Reading List – This is Kolbe Academy's biggest selling item, and with good reason. Visit www.kolbe.org or call (707) 255-6499 for a catalog. Simple, yet helpful, list.

A, ✠

Honey for a Child's Heart (Fourth Edition) by Gladys Hunt – This book has been around for decades and updated several times. I first read *Honey for a Child's Heart* when my children were very little and it inspired me to make the commitment to read aloud to them on a daily basis.

A

Honey for a Teen's Heart: Using Books to Communicate with Teens by Gladys Hunt and Barbara Hampton –

Mrs. Hunt writes about how to help your teen discern between good and bad books. She includes a reading list of over 300 books. It's nice to have a book that is written solely with teenagers in mind.
H, A

How to Read a Book by Mortimer Adler – This is the perfect book to give a student going off to college, or a high school student who is serious about receiving a good liberal arts education. Originally published in 1940, it's a guide to reading comprehension. You're taught the various levels of reading, reading techniques, and how to analyze, among other things.
H, A

*A **Mother's List of Books*** by Theresa Fugan – Theresa is a Catholic homeschooling mother and has personally reviewed the books on her list. Her literary suggestions are separated by age group and ordered by authors' last names. Order from Emmanuel Books (see appendix)
A, ✠

The Read Aloud Handbook by Jim Trelease – I love that Trelease promotes reading aloud in classrooms. He backs up his thesis with both statistical and anecdotal evidence. A thoroughly secular book, I don't agree with several of his book suggestions. However, it's still well worth the read.
A

Real Learning: Education in the Heart of the Home by Elizabeth Foss [By Way of Family] – Mrs. Foss does an excellent job in showing Catholic parents how they can implement Charlotte Mason's educational model into their homes. She distinguishes between "twaddle" and living books. Excellent reading list in the back, by grade level, but only through eighth grade.
A, ✠

A Student's Guide to Literature **(ISI Guides to the Major Disciplines)** by R. V. Young – This slender book is a guide to Western literature. Includes brief biographies and reading lists to introduce young college students to the classics. I would also recommend this book to an upper level high school student.
H, A

The Well-Educated Mind: A Guide to the Classical Education You Never Had by Susan Wise Bauer - Written to help adults educate themselves through reading the classics. Mrs. Bauer shows her readers how to improve their reading skills and set up a reading schedule. If you can find *Catholic Lifetime Reading Plan* by Father John Hardon [out of print], it's the perfect accompaniment to this book. I would replace some of Mrs. Bauer's suggested reading with Fr. Hardon's. Remember, if you want your children to grow up to be readers, you need to set the example.
A

Whigs and Tories: An American Revolution Reading List by Elizabeth Yank - The ultimate reading list for the American Revolution with over 350 titles, divided by reading level. Also includes a helpful introduction, timeline, commentary on the Catholic impact, and a list of Catholic text and reference books. Craft and activity books are also included. Email RPYank@juno.com for ordering information.
A, ✠

At a Glance

This reading list is for when you need a book in a hurry.

Preschool
Music
Ah, Music! by Aliki
Jazzy Alphabet by Sherry Shahan
Ludwig Van Beethoven (Getting to Know the World's Greatest Composers) by Mike Venezia
Art
A Child's Book of Prayer in Art by Sister Wendy Beckett
I Spy a Lion: Animals in Art by Lucy Micklethwait
A Boy Named Giotto by Peolo Guarnieri
Math
Wild Fibonacci: Nature's Secret Code Revealed by Joy Hulme
Domino Addition by Lynette Long, Ph.D.
Pigs in a Blanket: Fun with Math and Time by Amy Axelrod
Science
What's Smaller than a Pygmy Shrew? by Robert E. Wells
Everybody Needs a Rock by Byrd Baylor
A Tale of Peter Rabbit by Beatrix Potter
History
Noah and the Ark by Tomie dePaola
Jonah and the Great Fish by Clyde Robert Bulla
Song of the Swallows by Leo Politi
The Story of Johnny Appleseed by Aliki

First Grade
Music
DK Read and Listen: Illustrated Book of Ballet Stories by Barbara Newmann
Ella Fitzgerald: The Tale of a Vocal Virtuosa by Andrea

and Brian Pinkney
John Coltrane's Giant Steps by Chris Raschka
Art
A Child's Book of Art: Great Pictures First Words by Lucy Micklethwait
Leonardo and the Flying Boy: A Story About Leonardo Da Vinci by Laurence Anholt
Michelangelo (Getting to Know the World's Greatest Artists) by Mike Venezia
Math
Anno's Magic Seeds by Mitsumasa Anno
Grandfather Tang's Story: A Tale with Tangrams by Ann Tompert
Marvelous Math: A Book of Poems edited by Lee Bennett Hopkins and Rebecca Davis
Science
How to Dig a Hole to the Other Side of the World by Faith McNulty
Greg's Microscope by Millicent E. Selsam
The Moon Seems to Change by Franklin M. Branley
History
Pyramid by David Macaulay
The Egyptian Cinderella by Shirley Climo
Tut's Mummy Lost – And Found (Step-Into-Reading, Step 4) by Judy Donnelly
The Children's Book of America edited by Bill Bennett

Second Grade
Art
Brother Joseph: The Painter of Icons by R. Augustine DeNoble [Bethlehem]
Rembrandt (Getting to Know the World's Greatest Artists) by Mike Venezia
Math-terpieces by Greg Tang

Music

Johann Sebastian Bach (Getting to Know the World's Greatest Composers) by Mike Venezia

George Handel (Getting to Know the World's Greatest Composers) by Mike Venezia

Mr. Bach Comes to Call (Classical Kids) – audio drama

Math

How Much is a Million? by David M. Schwartz

What's Your Angle Pythagoras? A Math Adventure by Julie Ellis

The Librarian Who Measured the Earth by Kathryn Lasky

Science

Archimedes and the Door of Science by Jeanne Bendick

Watching Water Birds by Jim Arnosky

Catholic Stories from Science 2 by Nancy Nicholson [Catholic Heritage Curricula]

History

D'Aulaire's Book of Greek Myths by Ingri and Edgar d'Aulaire

How We Learned the Earth is Round by Patricia Lauber

The Trojan Horse: How the Greeks Won the War (Step-Into-Reading, Step 5) by Emily Little

Stories of Great Americans for Little Children (Lost Classics) by Edward Eggleston

Third Grade

Art

The Glorious Impossible by Madeleine L'Engle

The Boy Who Loved to Draw: Benjamin West by Barbara Brenner

What Makes a Goya a Goya? by Richard Muhlberger

Music

The Farewell Symphony by Anna Harwell Celenza

Beethoven (Famous Children) by Ann Rachlin

Mozart's Magic Fantasy (Classical Kids) – audio drama

Math
The History of Counting by Denise Schmandt-Besserat
One Grain of Rice by Demi
The Story of Money by Betsy Maestro
Science
==*Behold and See 3*== by Suchi Myjak [Catholic Heritage Curricula]
A Weed Is a Flower: The Life of George Washington Carver by Aliki
Pasteur's Fight Against Microbes (Science Stories) by Beverly Birch and Christian Birmingham
History
City: A Story of Roman Planning and Construction by David Macaulay
Julius Caesar by Robert Green
==*A Life of Our Lord for Children*== by Marigold Hunt [Sophia]
On the Mayflower by Kate Waters

Fourth Grade
Art
Katie Meets the Impressionists by James Mayhew
Degas and the Little Dancer: A Story About Edgar Degas by Laurence Anholt
Camille and the Sunflower: A Story About Vincent Van Gogh by Laurence Anholt
Music
Schubert (Famous Children) by Ann Rachlin
Chopin (Famous Children) by Ann Rachlin
Tchaikovsky Discovers America (Classical Kids) – audio drama
Math
On Beyond a Million: An Amazing Math Journey by David M. Scwartz
Math Curse by John Scieszke

The Confe$$ion$ and $ecret$ of Howard J. Fingerhut by Esther Hershenhorn

Science

Find the Constellations by H. A. Rey

Thomas Alva Edison: Young Inventor (Easy Biography) by Louis Sabin

The Man Who Made Time Travel by Kathryn Lasky

History

Made in China: Ideas and Inventions from Ancient China by Suzanne Williams

The Silk Route: 7,000 Miles of History by John S. Major

Leif the Lucky by Ingri and Edgar d'Aulaire

St. Martin de Porres by Mary Fabyan Windeatt [TAN]

Fifth Grade

Art

What Makes a Leonardo a Leonardo? by Richard Muhlberger

What Makes a Raphael a Raphael? by Richard Muhlberger

What Makes a Bruegel a Bruegel? by Richard Muhlberger

Music

The World's Very Best Opera for Kids . . . In English – audio CD

The Barefoot Book of Stories from the Opera by Shahrukh Husain and James Mayhew

Of Swans, Sugarplums, and Satin Slipper: Ballet Stories for Children by Violette Verdy

Math

Melisande by E. Nesbit

The Dot and the Line: A Romance in Lower Mathematics by Norman Juster

Sir Cumference and the First Round Table by Cindy Neuschwander

Science

Galen and the Gateway to Medicine by Jeanne Bendick

[Bethlehem]

Marie Curie's Search for Radium (Science Stories) by Beverly Birch and Christian Birmingham

Marconi's Battle for Radio (Science Stories) by Beverly Birch and Christian Birmingham

History

Son of Charlemagne (Living History Library) by Barbara Willard [Bethlehem]

St. Thomas Aquinas: The Story of the Dumb Ox by Mary Fabyan Windeatt [TAN]

The Door in the Wall by Marguerite DeAngeli

Priest on Horseback: Father Farmer, 1720-1786 by Eva Betz [Neumann]

Sixth Grade

Art

Michelangelo by Diane Stanley

What Makes a Rembrandt a Rembrandt? by Richard Muhlberger

What Makes a Picasso a Picasso? by Richard Muhlberger

Music

Bach (Famous Children) by Ann Rachlin

Handel (Famous Children) by Ann Rachlin

Vivaldi's Ring of Mystery (Classical Kids) – audio drama

Math

The Phantom Tollbooth by Norman Juster

G is for Googol: A Math Alphabet Book by David Schwartz

Anno's Mysterious Multiplying Jar by Masaichiro and Mitsumasa Anno

Science

Liquid and Gases: Principles of Fluid Mechanics by Paul Fleisher

Relativity and Quantum Mechanics: Principles of Modern Physics by Paul Fleisher

Waves: Principles of Light, Electricity, and Magnetism by Paul Fleisher

History

Fine Print: A Story About Johann Gutenberg by Joann J. Burch

The Children's Shakespeare by E. Nesbit

Outlaws of Ravenhurst by Sister M. Imelda Wallace, SL [Lepanto]

Never Turn Back: Father Serra's Mission by Jim Rawls

Seventh Grade

Art

Linnea in Monet's Garden by Christina Bjork

What Makes a Degas a Degas? by Richard Muhlberger

What Makes a Cassatt a Cassatt? by Richard Muhlberger

Music

Beethoven Lives Upstairs (Classical Kids) – audio drama

The Story of Hayden (Music Masters) – audio biography

The Story of Mozart (Music Masters) – audio biography

Math

The Adventures of Penrose the Mathematical Cat by Theoni Pappas

The I Hate Mathematics! Book by Marilyn Burns

A Gebra Named Al: A Novel by Wendy Isdell

Science

Matter and Energy: Principles of Matter and Thermodynamics by Paul Fleisher

Social Life in the Insect World by Jean-Henri Fabre

Isaac Newton and Gravity (Science Discoveries Series) by Steve Parker

History

The Flying Ensign: Greencoats Against Napoleon by Showell Styles [Bethlehem]

St. Pius: The Farm Boy Who Became Pope (Vision Book) by Walter Dietheim, OSB [Ignatius]

The Good Master by Kate Seredy
Johnny Tremain by Esther Forbes

Eighth Grade
Art
Art Through Faith by Mary Lynch and Seton Staff [Seton Educational Media]
What Makes a Van Gogh a Van Gogh? by Richard Muhlberger
First Impressions: Francis Goya by Ann Waldron
Music
Brahms (Famous Children Series) by Ann Rachlin
Tchaikovsky (Famous Children Series) by Ann Rachlin
The Story of Schubert (Music Masters Series) – audio biography
Math
String, Straight-Edge, & Shadow: The Story of Geometry by Julia E. Diggins
The Number Devil: A Mathematical Adventure by Hans Magnus Enzensberger
Fractals, Googols and Other Mathematical Tales by Theoni Pappas
Science
The Benjamin Franklin Book of Easy and Incredible Experiments by Lisa Jo Rudy
1000 Years of Catholic Scientists by Jane Meyerhofer [Ye Hedge School]
The New Way Things Work by David Macauley
History
Ben and Me by Robert Lawson
George Washington by Ingri and Edgar d'Aulaire
An Enemy Among Them by Deborah DeFord
Kat Finds a Friend: A St. Elizabeth Ann Seton Story (Glory of America) by Joan Stromberg [Ecce Homo]

Ninth Grade
Art
I, Juan de Pareja by Elizabeth de Trevino
First Impressions: Leonardo Da Vinci by Richard McLanathan
First Impressions: Michelangelo by Richard McLanathan
Music
An Introduction to Gregorian Chant by Richard Crocker
Classical Music for Dummies by David Pogue and Scott Speck
Jazz 101 by John F. Szwed
Math
The Man Who Counted: A Collection of Mathematical Adventures by Malba Tahan
The Snark Puzzle Book by Martin Gardner
Whatever Happened to Penny Candy? (Uncle Eric Book) by Richard Maybury
Science
Creator and Creation by Mary Daly [Ye Hedge School]
The Mystery of the Periodic Table (Living History Library) by Benjamin D. Wiker [Bethlehem]
Fabre's Book of Insects by Jean-Henri Fabre
History
The Powder Monkey by George Galloway
Lincoln: A Photobiography by Russell Freedman
Up From Slavery by Booker T. Washington
Father Damien and the Bells (Vision Book) by Arthur and Elizabeth Sheehan [Ignatius]

Tenth Grade
Art
First Impressions: Rembrandt by Gary Schwartz
The Life of Moses (Art Revelations) by Neil Morris

At-a-Glace Reading List

Mathematical Quilts by Dian Venters and Elaine Krajenke Ellison

Music

Math and Music by Trudi Hammel Garland and Charity Vaughan Kahn

The NPR Curious Listener's Guide to Classical Music by Tim Smith

Homegrown Music by Stephanie Ledgin

Math

Algebra Unplugged by Ken Amdahl

Sacred Geometry (Wooden Book) by Miranda Lundy

The Motley Fool Guide to Investing for Teens by David and Tom Gardner with Selena Maranjian

Science

Cartoon Guide to the Environment by Larry Gonick

Sun, Moon and Earth (Wooden Book) by Robin Heath

The Sand Reckoner by Gillian Bradshaw

History

Teen Guide to the Bible by Alfred McBride, O. Praem. [Our Sunday Visitor]

Shadow Hawk by Andre Norton [Bethlehem]

The Right Way to Live: Plato's Republic for Catholic Students by Richard Geraghty [CMJ Marian]

Commentaries on the Gallic War by Julius Caesar

Eleventh Grade

Art

First Impressions: Edgar Degas by Susan E. Meyers

First Impressions: Monet by Ann Waldron

The Life of Jesus (Art Revelations) by Neil Morris

Music

Classical Music 101 by Fred Plotkin

What to Listen for in Music by Aaron Copland

The NPR Curious Listener's Guide to World Music by

Chris Nickson
Math
The Cartoon Guide to Statistics by Larry Gonick
Li: Dynamic Form in Nature (Wooden Book) by David Wade
Economics in One Lesson by Henry Hazlitt
Science
Copernicus, Galileo, and the Catholic Sponsorship of Science by Jane Meyerhofer [Ye Hedge School]
Cartoon Guide to Genetics by Larry Gonick
Essential Elements: Atoms, Quarks, and the Periodic Table (Wooden Book) by Matt Tweed
History
Citadel of God by Louis de Wohl [Ignatius]
The Trumpeter of Krakow by Eric P. Kelly
Lepanto by G. K. Chesterton [Ignatius]
The Song at the Scaffold by Gertrude von Le Fort [Sophia]

Twelfth Grade
Art
Rome: Art and Architecture by Marco Bussagli, ed. [Konemann]
Sister Wendy's Story of Painting by Sister Wendy Beckett [DK]
Stopping Time by Gus Kayafas and Estelle Jussim
Music
Opera 101 by Fred Plotkin
The NPR Guide to Building a Classical CD Collection by Ted Libbey
The NPR Curious Listener's Guide to American Folk Music by Kip Lornell
Math
Calculus for Cats by Ken Amdahl
The Mathematical Experience by Philip Davis and Reuben

Hersh
Basic Economics: A Citizen's Guide to the Economy by
Thomas Sowell
Science
Life is a Blessing by Clare Lejeune [Ignatius]
*Darwin's Black Box: The Biochemical Challenge to
Evolution* by Michael Behe
Cartoon Guide to Physics by Larry Gonick
History
Uncle Tom's Cabin by Harriet Beecher Stowe
The Grapes of Wrath by John Steinbeck
The Hiding Place by Corrie ten Boom
An American Life by Ronald Reagan

College
Art
Notebooks of Leonardo Da Vinci
Ansel Adams: An Autobiography
In the Footsteps of Popes by Enrico Bruschini
Music
The Inner Game of Music by Barry Green
Who's Afraid of Classical Music by Michael Walsh
The NPR Curious Listener's Guide to Blues by David
Evans
Math
A History of Mathematics by Carl B. Boyer
Platonic and Archimedean Solids (Wooden Book) by
David Sutton
The Road to Serfdom by F. A. Hayek
Science
Chesterton: A Seer of Science by Stanley Jaki
On the Revolutions of Heavenly Spheres by Copernicus
The Universe in a Nutshell by Stephen Hawking
History
The Founding of Christendom (History of Christendom,

Vol. 1) by Warren Carroll [Christendom]
Democracy in America by Alexis de Tocqueville
The Roosevelt Myth by John T. Flynn
The Path to Power (The Years of Lyndon Johnson, Vol. 1)
by Robert Caro

Adult
Art
The Annotated Mona Lisa by Carol Strickland
*Heavenly City: The Architectural Tradition of Catholic
Chicago* by Denis McNamara [Liturgy Training]
In Tiers of Glory by Michael S. Rose
Music
The Vintage Guide to Classical Music by Jan Swafford
The NPR Curious Listener's Guide to Opera by William
Berger
The NPR Curious Listener's Guide to Popular Standards
by Max Morath
Math
*Uncle Petros and Goldbach's Conjecture: A Novel of
Mathematical Obsession* by Apostolos Doxiadis
Math: Facing an American Phobia by Marilyn Burns
The Worldly Philosophers by Robert Heilbroner
Science
*Keeping a Nature Journal: Discover a Whole New Way of
Seeing the World Around You* by Clare Walker Leslie and
Charles E. Roth
Miracles and Physics by Stanley Jaki [Christendom]
*On the Shoulders of Giants: The Great Works of Physics
and Astronomy* edited by Stephen Hawkings
History
How the Irish Saved Civilization by Thomas Cahill
How the Catholic Church Built Western Civilization by
Thomas E. Woods [Regnum]
The Power Broker: Robert Moses and the Fall of New York

by Robert Caro

The Politically Incorrect Guide to American History by Thomas E. Woods

Notes:

Appendix

Websites

Reading Lists

State-by-State Reading List
http://www.love2learn.net/literature/booklists/statread.htm
Great list if you'd like to tie geography into your literature lessons. Find out where the action takes place in the plot line and then find it on the map. This reading list sorts literature geographically by state. Look for links to literature sorted by countries.

100 Good Books List
www.classical-homeschooling.org/celoop/100.html
Reading list for adults. Provided by the Classical Christian Education Support Loop.

1000 Good Books List
www.classical-homeschooling.org/celoop/1000.html
John Senior's reading list for primary school through high school. Provided by the Classical Christian Education Support Loop.

Before Five in a Row
www.fiveinarow.com/before/booklist.html
Great literature list for preschool, whether you use Five in a Row curriculum or not.

Beyond Five in a Row
www.fiveinarow.com/beyond/booklist.html
Great literature list for upper grade school, whether you

use Five in a Row curriculum or not.

A Child's Reading List
www.eagleforum.org/educate/1995/sept95/ersept6.html
Provided by *The Education Reporter*. Sorted by reading level within genre.

Five in a Row
www.fiveinarow.com/fiar/booklist.html
Great literature list for grade school, whether you use Five in a Row curriculum or not.

Ten Books Every Student Should Read in College
www.humaneventsonline.com/article.php?id=743
A panel of twenty-eight scholars and university professors served as judges to develop this reading list.

Reading Your Way through History
www.readingyourwaythroughhistory.com
Alicia Van Hecke's terrific chronological reading list.

Seton Home Study School
www.setonhome.org/sitemap.stm
Seton's list of great books, for kindergarten through eighth grade to supplement their Catholic home study school. Scroll down to "reading lists."

Sonlight Books and The Well Trained Mind
www.nikkisbooknook.com/home/slwtm.html
Sonlight books arranged by *The Well Trained Mind*'s four-year cycles.

The Ultimate Reading List: Classics That Endure
www.eagleforum.org/educate/1997/june97/list.html
From *The Education Reporter*.

Literature Helps

Author Birthdays
www.waterborolibrary.org/birth.htm
Author birthdays by the month. Would be fun to have your students celebrate the birth dates of favorite authors.

Carol Hurst's Children's Literature Site
www.carolhurst.com
Book reviews and ideas on implementing literature in the classroom.

Catholic Educator's Resource Center
www.catholiceducation.org/
Articles and links of interest to Catholic educators.

Dinah Zike
www.dinahzike.com
Ideas for hands-on activities that can compliment literature studies.

Literature Based Reading Lessons
http://www.gardenofpraise.com/lesson.htm
Free literature-based reading lessons and unit studies. Created by teachers at a Christian school.

Literary Characters Clipart
http://etc.usf.edu/clipart/galleries/literature/literary_characters.htm
Use with reports, lap books, folders, and other displays.

MacBeth's Opinion
www.charlottemason.tripod.com
MacBeth Derham's literature suggestions for every subject.

Living Math
www.livingmath.net
Extensive literature list for mathematics, from preschool to college level.

Love 2 Learn
www.love2learn.net
Loads of book reviews. This is one of my favorite websites – very useful.

Used Books

Abebooks
www.abebooks.com
Inexpensive used book vendor

Bookfinder
www.bookfinder.com
Searches several used book vendors to find your selection.

CathSwap
www.groups.yahoo.com/group/cathswap/
A place to buy and sell used Catholic books and texts.

Homeschool Swap
http://groups.yahoo.com/group/homeschoolbookswap/
Trade Catholic homeschool materials or give away for the price of postage.

Homeschool Unlimited Classified
http://www.hsunlimited.com/classifieds/
Bulletin board to advertise used books for sale or to purchase.

Homeschooling Used Curriculum Sites
www.geocities.com/Athens/8259/used.html
Loads of links to websites and discussions groups for the
purpose of buying and selling used homeschooling books
and curricula.

My Homeschool Store
www.myhomeschoolstore.com/
Buy and sell curricula.

School Book Auction
http://www.schoolbookauction.com/
The eBay of homeschooling books.

Email Groups

Catholic Charlotte Mason
www.groups.yahoo.com/group/CatholicCMason/
Discussion group for Catholics using Charlotte Mason's
educational philosophy in their homeschool.

Catholic Classical Education
http://groups.yahoo.com/group/cce/
Discussion group for Catholics using a classical approach
in their homeschool.

The History Place
http://groups.yahoo.com/group/TheHistoryPlace/
History discussion group for Catholic homeschoolers.

Homeschool Library Connection
http://groups.yahoo.com/group/HomeschoolLibraryConnec
tion/
Help for homeschoolers who want to impact their library's
purchasing decisions.

Literature Alive
http://groups.yahoo.com/group/LiteratureAlive/
A place for Catholic homeschoolers to discuss literature and its place in their homeschools.

Living Math
http://groups.yahoo.com/group/LivingMathForum/
Non-sectarian discussion group for homeschoolers using "real books" in teaching math.

Pope St. Nicholas
http://groups.yahoo.com/group/PopeSaintNicholasV/
Help for Catholics who want to impact their library's purchasing decisions.

Blogs

Cajun Cottage
www.caygibson.typepad.com/cays_cajun_cottage/
Cay Gibson, author of *Catholic Mosaic*, blogs on children's literature.

Here in the Bonny Glen
www.melissawiley.net/
Children's author Melissa Wiley blogs on literature.

Homeschools and Libraries
www.homeschoolingandlibraries.wordpress.com/
Librarian and author Adrienne Furness writes on how homeschoolers and librarians can work together.

Love 2 Learn Blog
www.love2learnblog.blogspot.com/

Reviews of books and texts relevant to Catholic home-schoolers.

Maureen Wittmann
www.maureenwittmann.blogspot.com

Unity of Truth
www.unityoftruth.blogspot.com
Math and science blog for Catholic homeschoolers.

Contact Information

Catholic Publishing Houses

Most of the Catholic books found in the literary guides are from the following publishers:

www.chesterton.org
The American Chesterton Society
Publishes books by and about G. K. Chesterton
(952) 831-3096

www.ascensionpress.com
Ascension Press
The Great Bible Adventure.
(800) 376-0520

www.bethlehembooks.com
Bethlehem Books
Children's books and historical fiction.
(800) 757-6831

www.catholictextbookproject.com
Catholic Textbook Project
History and social studies textbooks.

Catholic World History Timeline and Guides
SMAcademy@aol.com
Marcia Neill
4790 Irvine Blvd., Ste. 105, Irvine, CA 92620

www.christendom.edu/press
Christendom College Press / ISI
Catholic books including Warren Carroll's books.
(540) 636-2900

www.eccehomopress.com
Ecce Homo Press
American Catholic historical fiction.
(866) 305-8362

www.hillsideeducation.com
Hillside Education
Literature guides and study helps.
Margot Davidson
475 Bidwell Hill Road
Lake Ariel, PA 18436

www.ignatius.com
Ignatius Press
Catholic books and videos, including religious curricula.
(800) 651-1531

www.olvs.org
Lepanto Press
Reprints of old favorites. Publishing house of Our Lady of Victory Home Study School.
(208) 773-7265

www.loyolabooks.org
Loyola Press
Publishers of Loyola Classics
(800) 621-1008

www.neumannpress.com
Neumann Press
Beautifully bound Catholic reprints.
(800) 746-2521

www.osv.com
Our Sunday Visitor

Catholic books and periodicals.
(800) 348-2440

www.pauline.org
Pauline Books & Media

Children's books and religious curriculum.
(800) 876-4463

www.booksforcatholics.com
Roman Catholic Books
Reprints Catholic classics.

www.setonhome.org
Seton Educational Media
Publishing house of Seton Home Study School.
(540) 636-9990

www.stpaulspub.com
St. Paul's Publishing
Our Roman Roots and *Evangelization of the New World.*

www.tanbooks.com
TAN Books and Publishers
Books and textbooks, both new and reprints.
(800) 437-5876

www.historylinks.info
Wooly Lamb Publishing
History Links Unit Study/Integrated Learning.
(360) 263-6568

www.hedgeschool.homestead.com
Ye Hedge School
Catholic science and sentence diagramming books.

Mary Daly
24934 478 Ave.
Garretson, SD 57030

Young Sparrow Press
Catholic children's books.
Box 265, Worcester, PA 19490
(215) 997-0791

Homeschooling Mail Order Companies

Appendix

www.adoremusbooks.com
Adoremus Books
(888) 392-1973

www.chcweb.com
Catholic Heritage Curricula (CHC)
(800) 490-7713

www.emmanuelbooks.com
Emmanuel Books
(800) 871-5598

www.writing-edu.com/
Institute for Excellence in Writing
(800) 856-5815

www.ourfathershouse.com
Our Father's House
(206) 725-0461

www.rchistory.com
Roman Catholic History
(877) 832-5829

About the Author

Maureen Wittmann and her husband Rob are home-schooling parents of seven children. She is coeditor and contributing author of *The Catholic Homeschool Companion* [Sophia Institute Press] and *A Catholic Homeschool Treasury* [out of print]. Her articles have appeared in *Heart & Mind, Our Sunday Visitor, Catholic Digest, Catholic Faith, New Covenant, Catholic Home Educator, Latin Mass*, and others. She has a weekly column at www.catholicexchange.com. You can visit her website at www.maureenwittmann.com and her blog at www.maureenwittmann.blogspot.com.

Please don't hesitate to contact Maureen at maureen@maureenwittmann.com, should you find a book listed in the literary guides that has gone out of print. Also, she'd love to hear about any books you think should have been included in *For the Love of Literature*. She'll note the titles on her blog and consider them for any future editions.

NOTES: